MW01077226

Tudor Style

Tudor Style

Tudor Revival Houses in America from 1890 to the Present

Text by **Lee Goff**

Photography by **Paul Rocheleau**

UNIVERSE

First published in the United States of America in 2002
by UNIVERSE PUBLISHING
A Division of Rizzoli International Publications, Inc.
300 Park Avenue South, New York, NY 10010

© 2002 Universe Publishing

Text © 2002 Lee Goff
All photos for the book © Paul Rocheleau, except for those photos on
the following pages:

© A. F. Kersting: page 12 (right), page 14 (right), page 17 (left and right),
page 18 (left), page 19 (right), page 21 (left)

© Arcaid: pages 13–14 (photo by Lucinda Lambton), page 18 (right, photo by
Richard Bryant), page 19 (left, photo by Lucinda Lambton), page 20 (right,
photo by Richard Bryant), page 21 (photo by Martin Jones)

© Country Life Magazine: page 20 (left and center)

© The National Photographic Library: page 12 (left, photo by Rob Matheson),
page 12 (center, photo by John Blake), page 13 (left and right, photos by
Rupert Truman), page 14 (left, photo by Matthew Antrobus)

All rights reserved. No part of this publication may be reproduced,
stored in a retrieval system, or transmitted in any form or by any means,
electronic, mechanical, photocopying, recording, or otherwise, without
prior consent of the publishers.

2002 2003 2004 2005 2006 / 10 9 8 7 6 5 4 3 2 1

Designed by Claudia Brandenburg
Universe Editor: Terence Maikels
Copy Editor: Laura Magzis

Printed in China

Acknowledgments

NO COMPREHENSIVE WORK HAS BEEN PUBLISHED ON THE TUDOR Revival house in America. One source that was invaluable in writing this book was Gavin Edward Townshend's scholarly and well-written Ph.D. dissertation, *The Tudor House in America: 1890-1930*. His work has been a mainstay; it guided me in structuring the book as well as suggesting regional variations for some of the thousands of Tudor Revival houses that exist in this country. His dissertation can be obtained from University Microfilms International, 300 North Zeeb Road, Ann Arbor, MI 48106.

I am greatly indebted to those who generously gave their time to guide me through their towns and suburbs. Mrs. Edwin Cromey drove me along the wooded roads of Tuxedo Park. Pam graciously provided introductions to homeowners and arranged access for photography. I also owe special thanks to Bronxville Village historian Eloise Morgan, who was my guide there. Eloise edited Bronxville's Centennial volume, *Building a Suburban Village, Bronxville, New York, 1898-1998*, the source of much of the information in the Bronxville section. She, too, took time to contact homeowners and provide introductions. They both have my profound gratitude for the time they took from busy schedules and for their warmth and kindness.

Realtors were often excellent sources, leading me to particular Tudor Revival houses and to individuals who could supply additional information. In Shaker Heights, Marilyn McCullar, of Realty One, was particularly helpful, taking snapshots of several houses and also graciously offering her office as a base in Shaker Heights. To her I am most grateful. My thanks also to Gail Sussman of Fox & Roach Realtors in Jenkintown, Pennsylvania, and to Barry Sloane of Sotheby's in Beverly Hills, California.

Historical societies, museums, and planning departments were particularly helpful, their officials giving their time to talk to me and provide suggestions and history. I thank Peter Lapham of the Chestnut Hill Historical Society; Tony Wells of the Woodward Corporation; Peter Coutant of the City of Lake Forest Planning Department and Janice Hecht of the Lake Forest Historical Society; Esley Hamilton of the St. Louis County Department of

Parks and Recreation; Audra Bartley of the Planning & Development Department in Shaker Heights; and Leslie Alpert of the Mayor's Office in Mount Vernon, New York.

A special word of gratitude to Cathleen Thorne-Thompson who gave openly of her time and information and to Professor Randall Makinson who made useful suggestions regarding Pasadena.

Special thanks to all the homeowners who graciously allowed their houses and the interiors to be photographed in the book. Many kindly tolerated whatever inconvenience this may have caused. To them my gratitude and the hope that they know how much they contributed to the book.

Paul Rocheleau not only did the expert photography that so beautifully illustrates the book but also made knowledgeable suggestions. He has my gratitude for the pleasure it was to work with him.

I am indebted to Terence Maikels for his editorial assistance in the many details required to see the book through to publication. He was most helpful and cooperative and I thank him. John Cox read the historical section of the manuscript and made thoughtful comments and criticism for which he has my gratitude. Any errors of fact, however, are mine and not his.

I thank all those who were so very helpful.

PAUL ROCHELEAU WOULD ALSO LIKE TO EXTEND HIS THANKS TO the following for all their help with his photography shoots: Jack and June Stein (Milwaukee); Katja Henke (Blantyre Castle); Julie Sullivan, Georgia Gogel, Mr. & Mrs. Shaffer, and Jill Rappaport (Bronxville); Mark and Phaedra Ledbetter (Pasadena); Troy Evans (Los Angeles); Cheryl Weaver (Lake Arrowhead); Jana Christian (Stan Hywet Hall); Kevin O'Donnel, Francis and Alice Gross, Mr. and Mrs. Dolin, and Theodore and Elaine Long (Shaker Heights); Andrew and Betsey Rosenfield, John Pope, Greg and Linda Stroh, Craig and Jane Omtvedt, and William Hanley (Lake Forest); and Charles Markarian (Tuxedo Park). Kathleen Thorne Thomas (Pasadena), Peter Lapham (Chestnut Hill), and Pam Cromey (Tuxedo Park) were of a special help to this book.

Introduction

NO OTHER HISTORIC ARCHITECTURAL STYLE IN AMERICA HAS AS MANY ALTERNATIVE LABELS as Tudor Revival does: Elizabethan, Jacobean, Jacobethan, Queen Anne, Old English, Cotswold. Although there are variations on each of the terms, Tudor Revival has come to be accepted both in the academic community and generally for its immediate association with structures that take as their source of inspiration the medieval buildings of Tudor England. Their characteristics are such elements as steeply pitched gables and roofs covered in slate or imitation thatch, bays of casement windows of diamond-paned leaded glass, clustered chimney stacks, interiors of wood paneling and parged ceilings, and especially half-timbered and stuccoed façades.

Architectural historian Gavin Townsend, in his excellent monograph *The Tudor House in America* (1986), asked, "Why were so many thousands of American homes built in such a style? When and how did they become so popular?" The Tudor Revival developed in America between 1890 and 1930. The reasons for its development were both cultural and practical.

Culturally, it was patriotic—a style with roots in America's colonial past and even farther back in late-medieval Britain with its associations of aristocracy, genteel living, stability, and dynasty. At a time when America's cities were overflowing with Italians, Irish, Scandinavians, Eastern Europeans, and other (supposedly undesirable) immigrant groups, those born here, with an Anglo-American genealogy, sought to set themselves apart as suggested by the Tudor style.

The 1876 Centennial Exhibition helped to fuel an interest in both American colonial architecture and in British architecture of an earlier time. Those yearning for antiquity even greater than that of the colonial past turned to the architecture of the mother country. The publication of architectural histories with fine photographs, drawings, and scholarship showing architects and clients what sixteenth- and seventeenth-century houses looked like also promoted interest in the Tudor style. Its expensive materials—copper, slate, and stone—made it a symbol of economic and social status. For the richest Anglo Americans, associations with the landed gentry of their forefathers made Tudor seem the style especially appropriate to their station in life.

And it was practical. Tudor houses were flexible and easily adapted to such additions as garages, studios, and verandas. The house integrated with its site, rambling over uneven terrain, at home with rocks and trees and other natural vegetation, requiring little in the way of expensive formal gardens. Unlike the symmetrical designs of the Colonial period, rooms could be oriented as desired with windows placed wherever appropriate to take advantage of sunny exposures or views of the landscape without upsetting the architectural symmetry. Moreover, at a time when industrialization's dehumanizing effects were being felt, the Tudor style's handcrafted half-timbering construction appealed to the Arts and Crafts movement's anti-industrial ideal made popular by the writings of John Ruskin and William Morris.

The first authentic American versions of Tudor houses were built in the 1880s. Architectural historian Mark Alan Hewitt said of them, "Initially, Tudor houses were built by the wealthiest Americans—tastemakers in the late-Victorian era. These were powerful and often famous people, such as Stuart Duncan of Newport, members of the Elkins family in Philadelphia, Frank Seiberling of Dayton, Alexander W. Weddell of Richmond, and W. E. Aldred of Long Island, New York. The prestige of the early Tudor mansions they built rubbed off on the style."[i] In spite of the popularity of Colonial styles, that prestige eventually produced the thousands of Tudoresque houses—small, medium, and large—that can be seen today in suburbs from coast to coast.

Most Tudor Revival styles were drawn from humble medieval cottages. The cozy and romantic Cotswold style, for example, drew owners to its low doors and windows and thatched roofing. Architects found inspiration in the simplicity of its lines and the use of a single material such as stone. Some Tudor Revival houses borrowed from late medieval manors with intersecting gables, parapets, and beautifully patterned stone or brickwork. True half-timbering of medieval houses was the integral support of the structure, extending through the walls and infilled with lathe and stucco. In the nineteenth and twentieth centuries such authentic work was prohibitively expensive to reproduce. Thus, Tudor Revival houses suggested the original half-timbering with timbers simply veneered to the walls and interspersed with stucco or patterned brick or stone.

This book illustrates Tudor Revival houses built during the period of their greatest popularity: the last century. As the style occurred in various regions of the country, its interpretations developed regional variations. New construction in the style, as the last chapter of this book shows—with a magnificent Tudor house of the twenty-first century—proves that the features that made the Tudor style attractive to owners in the 1920s and 1930s—its informality and comfort—continue to be desirable. One has only to travel the hilly, winding roads of a suburb such as Bronxville, New York, to appreciate how asymmetrical Tudor houses fit within their landscape, seeming to be as much a part of it as the trees themselves. In addition, they speak of a craftsmanship quite different from that of today's often flimsy building practices. And, thanks to their quality, they have held up well both physically and in market value. Solidity and comfort are their message as well as a connection to a more romantic time. Indeed, according to a recent architectural web site that conducted a "Dream House" survey, those responding were drawn to the small diamond-paned windows and the half-timbering of Tudor and English country styles. Tudor houses ranked Number One.

Further evidence of a continuing interest in the style—indeed, perhaps proof of it—is this book. It has been written in response to the many requests of booksellers, customers, owners, and scholars who find that no individual volume has been published about the phenomenon that is the Tudor style in America.

English Tudor

IGHTHAM MOTE, KENT: *An early style timber-framed house, Ightham Mote was constructed in the 1340s.*

ALFRISTON CLERGY HOUSE, SUSSEX: *This timber-framed house, which was most probably originally built for a wealthy farmer, dates back to around 1350.*

ANNE OF CLEVES HOUSE, LEWES, EAST SUSSEX: *As part of her divorce settlement from Henry VIII, Anne of Cleves was given this timber-framed house in East Sussex.*

BRITISH ROOTS[i]

BEFORE TUDOR REVIVAL APPEARED IN AMERICA, IT HAD BEEN REVIVED IN ENGLAND. As was the case in the history of American architecture in general—from colonial times and the Georgian period through the Victorian era—a style developed first in England and later crossed the ocean. What was fashionable in England ultimately became the fashion in America.

Allen W. Jackson, in his 1912 book *The Half Timbered House*, explained that half-timbering did not come into being because stripes happened to be the fashion. For yeoman builders, "it was the simplest, easiest, and quickest way of getting a house, and fulfilled a few necessary requirements."[ii] The earliest houses were built by joining together at the top two curved tree trunks, or crucks, set a distance apart. The crucks were then stabilized by a cross beam so that the whole formed a letter A. A second such frame was set up a distance away and the two were joined by a roof beam. Studs were used to create walls and the spaces between were filled with some kind of mortar, thus creating the striped effect, sometimes referred to as black and white.

The Tudor style, so called because it developed during the reigns of the Tudor monarchs—Henry VII, Henry VIII, Edward VI, Mary, and Elizabeth I—emerged at a time when Englishmen no longer needed fortified castles. At the same time, the more fortunate were enjoying increasing wealth, the result of what historian Anthony Quiney called "the great Tudor price rise." As he perceived it, "From about 1520 the population began to rise, perhaps as a

LITTLE MORETON HALL, CHESHIRE: *With the earliest part of the building built in the fifteenth century, Little Moreton Hall is considered one of the classic examples of timber-framed houses in the Tudor era.*

The gatehouse for the main hall fronts the moat that encircles the grounds.

LITTLE MORETON HALL, CHESHIRE: *A knot garden extends behind the southern façade of the main building.*

consequence of improved standards of living, and the increased demands for food and goods attending this rise led to higher prices." New trading families thereby acquired wealth, while in addition, Henry VIII rewarded court favorites with lands and riches derived from his suppression of monasteries. In the ensuing economic expansion large landowners and wealthy merchants alike replaced castles with grand manor houses and country estates.[iii]

In such houses the fortress-like character of earlier times gave way to increased elegance and domesticity. While the great hall of castle architecture remained central, it became less important for living as more specialized rooms were added for dining, sleeping, and withdrawing. Rooms were fitted with linen-fold oak paneling, ceilings received rich plaster relief, and the use of furniture increased.

While the Tudor inflation primarily benefited the rich, the yeoman's lot also improved. Fixed overheads for both yeoman landowners and long-term leaseholders enabled both groups to benefit from the higher prices charged for their goods and services.[iv] Thus they were able to build more substantial houses.

By the fourteenth century English carpentry had come of age with craftsmen increasingly skilled in the use of materials. By the end of the late Middle Ages carpenters had transformed their use of wall studs from functional to decorative, creating elaborate patterns in diamond, herringbone, or starry effects. More and more people could afford to hire skilled craftsmen and the new carpentry soon spread to the houses of England's yeomanry.

PRECEDING PAGES: LITTLE MORETON HALL, CHESHIRE: *The elaborate woodwork and the dramatic roof gables, as seen here in the entrance way to the hall, are indicative of timber-framed style houses in Cheshire during the Tudor era.*

SPEKE HALL, MERSEYSIDE: *The diagonal timbering and quatrefoil panels of Speke Hall, built between 1490 and 1612, are characteristic of Tudor era timber-framed houses in Lancashire and Cheshire.*

GREAT DIXTER, SUSSEX: *Actually three houses combined as one, Great Dixter consists of a mid-fifteenth-century house joined to an early-sixteenth-century house by an addition that was built in 1912.*

Half-timbering developed primarily in the great forest districts of England—counties in the southeast and the west Midlands—where oak flourished, providing hard, durable wood. Houses framed with it are a characteristic part of the scenery in these areas.

Stonework—particularly the limestone of the sixteenth and seventeenth century cottages such as Cotswold—was beyond the means of the everyday builder for some time because of the expense of quarrying, transportation, and the skill needed for laying. However, in the Middle Ages peasants began to construct buildings using the stones, or moorstones, cleared from fields. Once prosperity allowed masonry skills to reach down from the levels of monumental castle architecture to yeoman dwellings, stone in all its variety characterized numerous small towns and villages such as those in the Cotswolds themselves, the Pennines, and Dartmoor where building stone was plentiful.[v]

Domestic architecture built during the Tudor dynasty ranged from grand manors to humble abodes. The vernacular yeoman buildings of half-timber, rustic stone, and thatched or tiled roofs was, Quiney explained, "the orally communicated local tradition of craftsmanship." In England it was "restricted to buildings of one tradition only, or more accurately, a series of interlinked local sub-traditions which were born in the Middle Ages, flourished in the sixteenth and seventeenth centuries and died in the Industrial Revolution." Quiney continued, "A remarkable feature of this particular tradition of building is that it existed at really humble levels, just as a vernacular language does, and moreover, with a rich variety of forms and an unprecedented ability to survive."[vi]

LYTES CARY, SOMERSET: *Five hundred years in building, Lytes Cary includes a chapel (on the far left, built around 1343), the Tudor Great Hall (built around 1450), and the Great Chamber (1533).*

Late additions of north and west wings were added in the eighteenth century.

TIMBER-FRAMED HOUSES, HEREFORDSHIRE, LOWER BROCKHAMPTON: *The village of Lower Brockhampton contains numerous houses such as these that date back to the fifteenth and sixteenth centuries and show the local tradition.*

That it was local was (and is) the hallmark of vernacular architecture: Skilled local craftsmen used local materials to construct similar dwellings that occurred frequently in the same locality. For these rustic cottages, aesthetic appeal was a consideration, but it was not paramount. That such dwellings exhibit great variety is due, rather, to a direct response to the particularly varied English landscape and climate to which craftsmen adapted as needed.[vii] In the eighteenth century the old ways succumbed due to the Industrial Revolution's new techniques and to manufactured materials brought in cheaply by canal.

REVIVAL OF TUDOR STYLE IN ENGLAND

In the late eighteenth and early nineteenth century, the effects of the Industrial Revolution virtually obliterated Old England. In architecture the Gothic style was revived, notably in Horace Walpole's *Strawberry Hill*, but it was not well suited to ordinary houses. Quiney described it as being "too hectic." In reaction, the plainer forms of the mid-nineteenth century Arts and Crafts movement, inaugurated by William Morris, developed. In the 1790s the Picturesque movement emerged. It stressed such qualities as roughness, variation, and irregularity.

Those encouraging the Arts and Crafts movement endorsed sixteenth- and seventeenth-century Tudor architecture because it embodied Picturesque qualities and was congenial to the natural landscape. Reinforcing this view, illustrated books of scholarship

DILLINGTON HOUSE, SOMERSET: *Built in the early sixteenth century, Dillington, once part of the Speke estate (see page 16), was later remodelled in the Jacobethan style in the 1830s.*

MUNSTEAD WOOD, SURREY: *This Tudor Revival house was designed by Sir Edwin Lutyens, a master British architect in Tudor Revival style, for famed garden designer Gertrude Jekyll.*

were published with beautiful architectural drawings depicting the manor houses and mansions of the earlier era. Tudor Revival, following on the heels of Gothic Revival, often merged Gothic and Tudor details. In the words of Gavin Townsend, "Tudor Revival did not arrive at once in pure form; it came on the coattails of the Gothic Revival and crept in little by little, beginning with the picturesque enlargements of original Tudor buildings in the 18th century, progressing with the Gothicized Tudor projects of the Regency era, and finally coming into its own in the 1830s."[viii] During that decade, impressively grand country houses were constructed in Tudor style.

Several reasons accounted for the attraction of Britons to the earlier Tudor style. As would happen later in America, popular novels by writers such as Sir Walter Scott gave the bygone era a romantic gloss. Another impetus for the revival of Tudor style—and one that would also reappear later in America—was the social and industrial upheaval occasioned by the Industrial Revolution. British trade-union organizing and labor strikes became regular occurrences. The gentry felt themselves under siege. Tudor dwellings, reminiscent of Shakespeare's England, had associations of a calmer, more genteel and romantic time. Society found comfort in the stability that such houses evoked. They beckoned as havens.

Practical reasons as well as sentimental ones enhanced the style's appeal. Unlike the Georgian style, which was conventionally formal and could not be added to haphazardly without upsetting its balance, asymmetrical Tudor architecture could spread organically in

DEANERY GARDENS, SONNING: *Built in 1899, this Lutyens-designed Tudor Revival is located in Deanery Gardens, Sonning, a garden district also designed by Lutyens.*

WIGHTWICK MANOR, STAFFORDSHIRE: *The timbering style in this extension of Wightwick Manor (built by Edward Ould in 1887 and extended in 1893) combined with a lower story of brick, created an archetype of Arts and Crafts*

Jacobethan style and helped launch a local movement of building mock Tudors.

the landscape. Various in sizes and shapes, Tudor forms could ramble across the terrain, projecting wings here and ells there in seemingly natural outgrowth, their broken skylines of gables, towers, and clustered chimneys repeating the irregularities of nature's own creations. Tall, perpendicular windows, often grouped in bays, flooded interiors with light and air while the style's spacious floor plans, centered on a great living hall, were more convenient for domestic life. Indeed, the attraction of the style was its difference from the classical designs of the past two centuries. Townsend quotes Nikolaus Pevsner, saying the growing preference for Tudor was connected with "the general desire of the coming Victorian Age for something of bolder variety, thicker relief, a more restless play of light and shadows and altogether more robustness than the Georgians could offer in classic or Gothic shapes."[ix] And finally, in addition to all its other virtues, Tudor architecture belonged. It originated in Britain.

Nevertheless, in spite of its virtues, Tudor Revival was eclipsed for a time by the Gothic style, championed particularly by A. W. Pugin, a Catholic who was devoted to the pointed style as associated with "Christian probity." When Tudor Revival reemerged in the 1860s as a popular style for British country houses, it found its sources not in the higher architecture of castles and manors but in the vernacular half-timbered forms that ultimately became important to the American Tudor Revival.[x]

Architects drew on dwellings of the Tudor period in designing cottages, vicarages, and farmhouses. Rustic primitiveness was one of the recurrent themes of the late eighteenth

LEYSWOOD, NEAR GROOMSBRIDGE: *Richard Norman Shaw's masterpiece, Leyswood, was built in 1868.*

LEYSWOOD, NEAR GROOMSBRIDGE: *The gatehouse to Shaw's Leyswood.*

MERRIOT WOOD, SURREY: *This interior view of Shaw's Merriot Wood displays the great height of the gabled ceiling.*

century's Romantic movement, and the Tudor cottage, so emblematic of the peasant, celebrated the simple life. For the gentry, fashion dictated a return to nature, a return to the country. What at first had been workers' cottages and other outbuildings constructed in Tudor style on large estates by the nineteenth century were being built as pleasure getaways for the rich seeking to escape the stresses of modern life. For what could be more appealing to the harried, well-to-do Briton than a charming rustic cottage nestled in bucolic landscape? Surely there one could get back to nature and find a less complicated life.[xi]

Tudor architecture with its flexibility and livability so suited the home-loving English that it continued in the British Isles indefinitely. John Ruskin, the Victorian era's most influential critic and devoted admirer of the Old English cottage, promoted it in his writing, and Richard Norman Shaw, one of the great designers of the Victorian vernacular revival, helped to perpetuate it.[xii]

One house in particular, Shaw's Leyswood, built in 1868, brought the Tudor style—or Queen Anne, as it was called—to the attention of Americans when it was published in *Building News* in 1871. The term *Queen Anne* is a somewhat confusing one, the source of some scholarly debate. The noted art historian Vincent Scully insisted, "Indeed, a better name for Shaw's early houses might be Elizabethan rather than Queen Anne," adding that it is undoubtedly a misnomer.[xiii] He argued that Leyswood and other early Shaw houses were charming pastiches. "If they inspired later original work in America and England, they also gave rise to thousands

KNIGHTSCROFT, RUSTINGTON: *Built in 1880–81, Shaw's Knightscroft is a later example of his work.*

MOCK TUDOR HOUSES: *In the twentieth century, "mock Tudor" houses became popular in many neighborhoods around England, as is demonstrated here by this line of interwar houses.*

of Tudor cottages both here and in England." Publications featured the semi-Tudor, half-timbered designs that ultimately influenced leading architects. Consequently," Scully said, "Wherever Americans might have looked in the pages of *Building News* during 1873 and 1874, they would have been faced by the brick, the half timber, and above all the tile hangings and leaded casements in generous banks, of the Queen Anne."[xiv]

Leyswood was a large house of late-medieval forms, many Tudoresque, but also including motifs that were more Gothic than Tudor. Its immediate appeal in both Britain and America was to a new and growing class of affluent commuters who were taken by its use of vernacular elements to provide a more livable residence than its size might otherwise suggest. Leyswood was not "high" Tudor. That is, it did not imitate a Tudor castle or manor. But, perhaps for that very reason, it exerted a profound influence.[xv] In time, as Tudor Revival houses came into their own, they would follow more scrupulously the English historical style. In the meantime, however, Queen Anne reigned in her rather more improvisational manner.

She did so, moreover, on both sides of the Atlantic, for many of the same factors that had caused the Tudor style's revival in England emerged to promote it in the United States, especially during the late nineteenth and early twentieth century. By the 1920s, in fact, the Tudor Revival had become a permanent part of domestic American architecture in the country's rapidly growing suburbs. But that was still years off.

Tudor in America

TUDOR REVIVAL AND SUBURBAN AMERICA

BY THE MIDDLE OF THE NINETEENTH CENTURY A REVOLUTION IN TRANSPORTATION WAS underway in America as railroads snaked their way into the countryside and opened up farmland to suburban residential development. By the turn of the century, transportation had shifted into high gear with the advent of the internal combustion engine. And by 1920, shortly after the end of World War I, Henry Ford was rolling his Model Ts off the production line at the rate of one every twenty seconds. The private automobile had arrived and would permanently alter American life, the American landscape, and American architecture.

Industrialization was the twofold catalyst for these developments, for it made the suburbs accessible while simultaneously creating conditions encouraging a desire to escape the cities. In the words of historian Leland Roth, "The idea of the romantic landscaped suburb had arisen parallel with the emergence of industrialization."[i] The flight to the countryside was led by the upper classes, but they were soon followed by the middle class, facilitated by the car and commuter trains. If the source of their wealth was the city, the country was where these people escaped the crowds and industrial blight that they had helped to create.

Suburban communities, many of them founded during the nineteenth century, grew rapidly around major cities. Between 1910 and 1940, New York's Tuxedo Park and Bronxville, Philadelphia's Chestnut Hill and Main Line, Cleveland's Shaker Heights, and Chicago's Lake Forest, among others, experienced their periods of greatest growth. During those years the suburban house, a major concern of the architectural profession, was at first designed with great eclectic freedom, generally drawing on Renaissance or medieval precedents, with Tudor elements preferred.[ii] This architectural expression, which first took hold in estates of industrial barons, in time would spread to the developing suburbs, along with another predominating style—Colonial.

EARLY INFLUENCES: 1835–70

Alexander Jackson Davis's pattern books for villas and cottages, published in the 1830s and 1840s and widely employed by builders, greatly influenced the Picturesque in America. Davis deplored traditional American domestic architecture and its classical styles. He was the first American architect to adopt Tudor-Gothic designs in his houses. In 1833 he designed Glen Ellen, a deliberately off-center house in Baltimore, for Robert Gilmore, a Scottish merchant enamored of the novels of Sir Walter Scott. In 1836, for William Paulding, Davis designed Lyndhurst in Tarrytown, New York, an essentially Gothic house, but with a prominent Tudor gable. In short, Davis initiated the Gothic Revival in America and, as Townsend explained, "as with the Gothic Revival in Britain, Tudor was sure to follow."[iii] Rather than confining his work to impressive villas, Davis also designed immensely popular Picturesque cottages in affordable wood instead of costly stone.

In 1838, Davis met Andrew Jackson Downing, an architectural critic, landscape designer, and promoter of the Picturesque in America whose writings virtually dictated fashion in American domestic architecture at that time. Downing helped to popularize Davis's designs and between 1840 and 1875, Davis's work succeeded in transplanting to America England's enthusiasm for Tudor.

Other pattern-book authors, such as Samuel Sloan and Marriott Field, popularized Tudor-derived designs for picturesque Old English cottages and Elizabethan villas. However, as Townsend observed, very few authentic Tudor Revival mansions were built before the Civil War, and what influence the pattern books had on Tudor Revival declined in the 1860s. What was needed was European influence and it would come through the previously mentioned designs of Richard Norman Shaw.[iv]

FURTHER INFLUENCES: 1870–90

An early practitioner of historical Tudor Revival architecture was Henry Hobson Richardson (1838–86), the outstanding figure in American architecture in the 1870s and 1880s. His reputation as America's most original architect was rivaled only by that of Frank Lloyd Wright. Richardson trained at the Ecole des Beaux Arts in Paris and traveled widely in England and on the Continent. When he began practicing after his return, he increasingly included Tudor and Picturesque elements in his designs, especially those for private residences. Most

Between 1910 and 1940, suburban communities grew rapidly around major cities. One such community was Shaker Heights, Ohio, where these two Tudor Revival houses can be found.

significant was the new sense of space that he developed by transforming the Tudor great hall into an open, informal living area, featuring entrance, fireplace, and stair and opening to adjoining rooms. As historian Vincent Scully observed, these open plans became the basis of modern architecture.[v] Adapting them from European medieval architecture, Richardson went on to interpret the interior planning and exterior forms—the towers, turrets, and arches—in such an innovative way as to make them a truly American style. Townsend speculates that Richardson was influenced by the drawings he saw of Richard Norman Shaw's Leyswood in the March 31, 1871 issue of *Building News*, perhaps brought to his attention by Stanford White of his firm.

White left Richardson's office, eventually becoming the White of the firm McKim, Mead & White in New York. That firm too would design many houses using the Old English vocabulary of gables and "living halls," but substituting wood shingles for the tiles of England. Their work in Americanizing Tudor took considerable liberties with the style, particularly in combining its elements with features derived from other styles as did other architects of the 1880s.

Tudor style made further advances in the American consciousness by means of the 1876 Centennial Exhibition in Philadelphia, celebrating the 100th anniversary of the nation's birth. Two British government buildings in the Old English cottage mode excited particular enthusiasm with their evocations of a "supposedly more virtuous and desirable past than the present,"[vi] as Vincent Scully put it. Essentially Elizabethan in character, they were built in a half-timbered style and referred to as Queen Anne. The *American Builder* gave these

At the same time that Tudor style houses were becoming popular in the late nineteenth / early twentieth centuries, French derivations of the Tudor style also crossed the Atlantic.

The Stein house, located just outside of Milwaukee demonstrates this French influence with its turrets, brickwork, and steep slate roofs. With timbering similar to Tudor architecture,

this house is often mistakenly regarded as Tudor architecture.

Tudor-related buildings a rave review, prompting Vincent Scully to later note , "Thus the rough and ready *American Builder*, champion of practicality and hardheadedness . . . fell head over heels in love with the Queen Anne in its most antiquarian aspect, the half-timbered."[vii]

"Acceptance of Queen Anne," Scully added, "depended in 1876 upon still another factor, which seems at first glance entirely unrelated, yet which became inseparably connected. As the Queen Anne purportedly revived vernacular English domestic architecture of several centuries past, it began to be related in the minds of Americans to their own colonial building of one hundred to two hundred years before." Scully then cited an editorial in *American Architect* discussing the failure of exhibition organizers to include an early American farmhouse in the United States Centennial display and noting that the British had built for their display two half-timbered structures of two centuries earlier. As Scully pointed out, "In the same breath with the discussion of New England farmhouses with a 'history' the *American Architect* mentions the English Queen Anne houses. The Queen Anne thus rode into America on a wave of nostalgia, and that nostalgia was a new and suddenly poignant American longing to recall its 17th and 18th century past. The longing became a powerful force in the early 1870s and culminated in the colonial enthusiasm aroused by the Centennial of 1876."[viii] The fair had created national fervor, but it had also brought to the attention of the American public British architecture of the sixteenth and seventeenth century, a period immediately preceding British settlement in North America and allied with it in the informality and simplicity of its domestic architecture.

Two examples of suburban Tudor Revival: a residence in Cincinnati, Ohio (left), and the Smith Pirie house in Lake Forest, Illinois (right).

TUDOR REVIVAL: 1890–1917

Toward the end of the nineteenth century increasing numbers of American architects traveled to Europe to enroll in the Ecole des Beaux Arts, the bastion of nineteenth-century classicism. At the same time, several architectural schools were founded in the United States with the same type of training. As Townsend said, "Inspiration and beauty was to be sought in forms permanent and proven." Students were encouraged to study books containing measured drawings of ancient monuments, if not travel to such wonders to do their own measurements and photograph and draw them. The result was a declining interest in eclectic designs combining elements from various eras. In their place emerged an interest in styles that more closely followed the originals. Two trends developed in domestic architecture: one followed classical design and the other looked to something more medieval. By the 1890s these two trends had prevailed.[ix]

In 1893, Chicago's World's Columbian Exposition helped to promote Colonial Revival, a style based on classical forms. The architects appointed by Daniel Burnham, the fair's planner, to design the various main buildings of the exhibition agreed early on that unity of expression was essential. To achieve it, the classical style had of necessity to be used as it was the only one they all knew equally well. Its buildings, classical and neo-classical Renaissance Revival, were pristine white and set against Chicago's gritty backdrop.

At the time, architects in general felt a need for a clearer sense of order in their work, as well as an architecture that would better adapt to modern living patterns. Many therefore turned to the security of historical and classical forms, hoping to find the new by adapting the old to new uses. In this way, while the exposition itself gave rise to a return to classical design, it also, like the 1876 Centennial, awakened an interest in America's colonial past. Colonial Revival, a style that borrowed heavily from early-American Georgian and Federal designs—likewise rooted in classical orders—became the vogue.

Thus developed the two revival styles that contested for popularity for many years to come, classical Colonial and late Medieval Tudor, which, in Scully's view, was closely connected in the public mind with America's beginnings. Colonial, appealing to nostalgia for a younger America, led in popularity. But Tudor, with its suggestion of English roots, was not far behind. Despite the suburb dwellers' preference for symmetrical and columned colonial styles, many of their neighbors yearned for greater antiquity. And architects continued to satisfy their needs.

In his 1912 book, *The Half Timbered House*, Allen W. Jackson declared, "In the half-timber houses of England were born, lived and died our own great-grandfathers; these houses were conceived and wrought out by our own progenitors; they are our architectural heritage, our homesteads, and hold an important place in our building history."[x]

Jackson was expressing a view widely held by Americans at the time. With waves of immigrants passing through Ellis Island, those born in America sought to set themselves apart from the foreign-born by proclaiming their (assumed) Anglo-American purity through the architecture of their houses. The Tudor house represented stability—indeed, intimations of dynasty. And for further justification, lest it be thought to be an imported style and thus an affectation, one could cite evidence that in New England, underneath the later external casings of early houses were actually half-timbered houses. A demonstrable connection was established between the two, because in early English houses, when the wood studs shrank and pulled away from the mortar filling, opening drafty spaces to the weather, these were then covered over by wood, tile, or plaster, thus disguising the half-timbering, but continuing the life of the structure.[xi]

During this period of classical and historicist design of houses, one architect, Frank Lloyd Wright, was developing his own vocabulary. To Wright, classical and revival styles had little to do with modern social patterns. Although he was working to move away from such work, early on he did occasionally succumb. With its strong gable trimmed with half-timber-like stripes, one of Wright's first houses, built in 1895 in Oak Park, a suburb of Chicago, is a simplified and somewhat abstract version of Tudor style. His abstracting of half-timbering continued and may be seen years later in the 1902 Ward Willitts house in Highland Park, Illinois.

From about 1890 until World War I, architects became interested in designing Tudor houses that were more historically accurate than the earlier designs of McKim, Mead & White

LEFT: *Frank Lloyd Wright's 1895 Moore house, Oak Park, Illinois, is an abstract version of Tudor Revival and one of the few he designed in the style.*

RIGHT: *The timbers between the windows of the 1902 Ward Willits house, Highland Park, Illinois, represent a culmination of Wright's experimentation with half-timber abstraction.*

and others of the period before 1890. Townsend says that "at one time or another nearly every turn-of-the-century American architect designed at least one Tudor Revival house." Among such architects' designs for important houses were Robert Swain Peabody's 1904 house for Percival Roberts in Narthberth, Pennsylvania, T. Henry Randall's 1898 Henry Poor house in Tuxedo Park, and John Russell Pope's 1914 design for Stuart Duncan in Newport, Rhode Island. Other architects of the period designing Tudor houses were Ralph Adams Cram and Bertram Goodhue.[xii] But it was not until the 1920s that the style would hit its stride.

TUDOR'S HEYDAY IN AMERICA, 1920s

A 1913 article in the *Architectural Record* illustrating the Tudor residence of Frederick F. Brewster in New Haven, Connecticut, gives a contemporary view of the demand for Tudor. Richard H. Dana Jr. in "A Study in the Tudor Style" said, "The adaptability of Tudor domestic architecture to country houses in America today has not often been advocated in theory and still less often established in fact." The article then discusses the style's "comfortable and cheerful features," stating that elements that made the interior attractive proved to be "effective and interesting on the exterior also." The article cites two reasons for the style's not yet becoming generally appreciated. First is the failure to distinguish the Tudor from the Victorian Gothic. Second is "our horror of the battlemented Hudson River Castles [from which we] have turned for refuge to the formality of the Renaissance styles, especially the popular stucco villas or colonial homesteads."

LEFT: *Tudor Era Cotswold-style houses with the local Wissahickon schist characterize Chestnut Hill and other Philadelphia suburban architecture.*

RIGHT: *Just outside Chestnut Hill in the Mount Airy neighborhood is this twin Tudor house. Built in the late 1920s for a doctor and his family, the house was divided into two halves* *to allow for separation between the doctor and his adult children.*

"But," the article asks, "is this classic spirit what the country dwellers themselves really want in their homes? Is not the Tudor informality just beginning to be appreciated and accomplished among us?"[xiii] In less than a decade, Tudor style would become the vogue for houses at all levels of housing from seaboard to seaboard.

For American magnates of the time—bankers, financiers, stockbrokers—Tudor houses carried aristocratic associations. In their suburbs the number of Tudor-style country clubs was almost as great as that of their Tudor houses. Social lives centered on these exclusive bastions, where member's lounges might be decorated with murals of British hunting scenes—gentlemen in hunting pinks riding to the hounds. Their "Men-Only" bars, from which the sounds of backgammon dice and the scent of cigars emanated, were paneled in dark oak. Their Tudor houses meanwhile were apt settings for book collections, hunting or riding gear, and, in general, the life of a country squire. Historian Mark Alan Hewitt noted, "Another strong image conveyed by Tudor houses was the cachet of expensive materials—copper, slate, and especially stone."[xiv] Tudor was so associated with economic achievement and conservative good taste that it was commonly known as "Stockbroker Tudor."

As had happened earlier in England, books with beautiful illustrations of sixteenth- and seventeenth-century manor houses included extensive spreads of noble country houses surrounded by typically informal English landscape. Gavin Townsend mentions other media: movie sets depicting charming Scottish villages of thatch-roofed cottages and best-selling novels

In the 1920s the popularity of Tudor-style architecture spread throughout America, including among the famous—and infamous. Mobster Bugsy Segal built this Tudor-style house for his growing gambling business. Named The Tudor House, an extension of the building was used as a brothel. Today, the building exists as a stylish bed and breakfast.

portraying, in Townsend's words, "the Elizabethan era as one of romance and vigor, when men were men, rulers were rulers, and . . . houses were houses."[xv]

Developers were quick to adopt the style in so-called garden communities. It was taken up throughout the country in middle-class suburbs, where thousands of Tudoresque houses with half-timbering, clustered chimney stacks, and a medieval aspect were built. Nor was the style limited to the private, single-family house. Developers chose Tudor for clusters of buildings in suburban communities like Forest Hills Gardens, Queens, and Chestnut Hill, near Philadelphia.

These communities, similar to the Hampstead Garden suburb in Greater London, developed in the twentieth century as a livable solution to high-density housing for urban populations. In Forest Hills, framing the Tudor-style plaza was an apartment development with residential towers above arcaded shops. Intended as middle-class housing, it became a community for the more affluent because of rising construction costs and demand for such solidly constructed housing.[xvi] In Chestnut Hill in 1916–17, George Woodward developed Cotswold Village as rental housing, using the ubiquitous local Wissahickon schist.

As the style of the grand American manor house in this way was assimilated into middle-class culture, mail-order catalogues broadcast the style anew through plans for single-family Tudor houses, although at a slower rate. No doubt this was because the elements of the style and its materials were more difficult to execute individually at low cost.

Tudor Revival houses characterize the residential architecture of Forest Hills streets.

DECLINE OF TUDOR

The suburban Tudor style had a run of nearly half a century, a long time considering the fickle nature of architectural taste. Perhaps the style had simply run its course. In any case, the Depression effectively ended it for all but those who had the wherewithal. Building costs were prohibitive as incomes plummeted. Given their pinched circumstances, the 1930s forced builders to forsake the half-timbering, leaded-glass windows, elaborate clustered chimneys, and other elements that made a house Tudor.

Modernism had also come to America in the early 20th century. In the late 1920s many writers and publications, favoring avant-garde modernism, criticized period-revival houses, especially Tudor. Townsend quotes a 1928 essay in *Architectural Forum* entitled "Houses or Stage Scenery," by H. V. Walsh, discussing and illustrating two Tudor houses: "We are going through a very strange period in our domestic architecture. It is a make-believe era. We seem to want to live in dream houses, in quaint, old-fashioned houses, in fantastic castles. Whatever . . . the cause of this feeling, the evidence is growing on every hand that people are demanding houses that reflect, not our own age, but some other past age. Ought we not frown on use of all those styles of architecture, which depend for effect on stage scenery, which imitates the work of the hand craftsman and the patina of age?"[xvii]

The modernist movement of the 1920s and 1930s rejected any and all historical references and ornament. In what came to be known as the International Style, it produced the modern villa with unadorned, crisp white walls and steel and all-glass façades. But mainstream America found such houses sterile. When building resumed after World War II, architects and their more conventional clients rejected this model, which generally failed to consider site, climate, and local materials. And so, while it is conjectural whether it was the direct influence of modernism that precipitated the decline of the Tudor style, undoubtedly modernism's interest in functionalism, plus prefabricated materials, contributed to the decline of Tudor construction.

Thereafter the Tudor did not resume its former popularity. Nevertheless, the houses that were built in the style before the war have become valuable real-estate properties. And as recently as 1989, a mail order company, Home Planners, Inc., published "A portfolio of floor plans, exteriors, and furnishing ideas for 80 enchanting Tudor houses," from cottages to villas to manors. The brochure proclaimed Tudor style to be "solid, substantial, and self-assured . . . one that generations of upwardly mobile Americans have consistently aspired to. From medieval times on, it has been a desired symbol of achievement, a live-in reward for effort, enterprise, and, eventually, success." The Tudor-style house is "not ancient architecture but living history. It is a recognition that tradition is not trapped in time but is something that remains relevant generation after generation."[xviii]

NEW YORK CITY SUBURBS

OPPOSITE PAGE: *Brook Farm, Tuxedo Park. Noted architect Donn Barber designed this extravagant complex for financier Richard Delafield. Although much of the complex was demolished, signs of its original use—training thoroughbred race horses—can be found in the 110-foot-long stables, since converted to eight wainscoted and pegged timber garage spaces.*

NO OTHER AREA CAN CLAIM MORE TUDOR HOUSES THAN THE COMMUNITIES SURROUNDING New York City. The number within commuting distance of Manhattan could fill a volume of its own—Garden City, Long Island; Teaneck and the Oranges in northern New Jersey; Forest Hills, Queens; and all of Westchester, to name a few. Across the country other city suburbs have their concentrations of Tudor houses, but nowhere else can boast the numbers that exist in the communities near New York City.

Westchester alone has thousands of such houses. The terrain is particularly suited to the asymmetrical, picturesque style. Heavily wooded, hilly, and marked by eruptions of rocky outcroppings, it is the kind of landscape for which the irregular architecture of the Tudor style is so suited. In addition, it was inevitable that Tudor became *the style* simply because these communities were developed during the years of Tudor's greatest popularity—1890 to 1930.

Westchester became increasingly accessible to New York City with the development of commuter railroads and new parkways—the railroads by the 1880s and the parkways by the mid-1920s. Real estate developers seized the opportunity, building houses as quickly as a city-dweller's automobile could drive up the Henry Hudson Parkway to reach his house. According to historian Gavin Townsend, the population of Westchester County in 1900 was 184,257; by 1920 it had doubled to 344,436; and by 1930 it was well over a half-million.[i]

Illustrating the houses in a few of these suburbs demonstrates the popularity of Tudor Revival as it occurred in the developing communities, rich and not so rich, within a commute of New York City.

FOLLOWING SPREAD, LEFT: *Julliard Carriage House, Tuxedo Park. This carriage house once belonged to one of the original residents of Tuxedo Park, Augustus D. Julliard, whose family sponsored the Julliard School of Music in New York City.*

FOLLOWING SPREAD, RIGHT: *Thomas Stokes House, Tuxedo Park. Built at the turn of the century, this house is referred to as an Elizabethan cottage, one of the many terms that Tudor encompasses. Like other Tudor houses in Tuxedo Park, the asymmetrical, vernacular style is ideally suited to its natural surroundings.*

Tuxedo Park
TUXEDO PARK, NEW YORK

THE EXCLUSIVE COMMUNITY OF TUXEDO PARK IS located about an hour from New York along the Ramapo River. In 1885 Pierre Lorillard, the tobacco magnate, purchased 7,000 acres, originally intending it as a hunting preserve for himself and his friends. But soon the original sporting purpose was abandoned for a more commercial real estate venture. Nevertheless, entrance to the park is no less restricted today than it was at its inception. A forbidding gatehouse of boulders piled in the manner of H. H. Richardson marks the entrance. Before being allowed to enter, visitors must pass guards who check to see the visitor is expected by the resident.

Subdivided into irregular wooded, rocky lots overlooking Tuxedo Lake, the properties are connected by winding, hilly roads. The chief planner was Ernest Bowditch, a landscape architect who was influenced by the work of Frederick Law Olmstead. Picturesque landscape required picturesque architecture. To design it, Lorillard commissioned Bruce Price as his chief architect. Price was equally well known in social and architectural circles. The social center for the residential section was a Price-designed stone clubhouse. Outside the gates he created a few commercial buildings and a railroad station. The first speculative cottages within the park were Shingle Style with some Tudor touches such as half-timbering, a style that Price brought to such perfection that Frank Lloyd Wright drew on Price's work for his own house in Oak Park, Illinois. Before long, however, the simple shingled

cottages were not grand enough for the new fortunes of the time. Affluent Americans made frequent transatlantic crossings and were impressed—and envious of—the grand European manor houses they saw. Price's unpretentious cottages were soon abandoned for lavish manors. In 1887 Price designed a large half-timbered house for Lorillard himself. That was followed in 1898 by an enormous Tudor mansion of stone built for Henry Poor, founder of Standard and Poor's rating service and a Wall Street speculator. One of the first residences in the monumental style, Poor's was a three-story Jacobean Tudor structure. Although other styles were represented, the Tudor style continued to shape the character of Tuxedo Park into the 1920s, both for its British associations of aristocracy and because it was so well suited to the irregular terrain and wooded sites.

However, Black Friday, October 29, 1929, struck. In the dark days of the Depression, with bankrupt owners unable to pay real estate taxes, many of the larger manor houses fell victim to demolition, were purposely set on fire, or were simply boarded up and became derelict. For a time, activity in Tuxedo quieted. Some of the great manors became educational or religious institutions. Henry Poor lost everything, including his fabulous mansion, once the showplace of Tuxedo Park. Poor's mansion ultimately became a religious retreat.

In the 1960s, prosperity brought younger families to the park. They acquired and restored many of the smaller, more manageable buildings—carriage houses, gardeners' cottages, old garages—giving Tuxedo Park added charm.

Today, caring owners have restored many of the mansions. Tuxedo has some of the finest examples of Tudor Revival architecture to be found.

Bronxville[ii]

THE STREETS OF SUCH WESTCHESTER SUBURBS AS Scarsdale, Pelham, Larchmont, and Bronxville are lined with Tudor houses, none more so than Bronxville, which is about twenty minutes by rail from New York.

Its early developer was William Van Duzer Lawrence (1842–1927). He had made his fortune marketing patent medicine in Canada and eventually moved to New York. In 1889, his brother-in-law told Lawrence about a plot of eighty-six acres in Bronxville—a ramshackle farm—that was for sale. Lawrence decided to invest, putting in $43,000. From his earlier business, he knew the value of promotion. He was so successful in putting it to use for his new development that by 1892, Mount Vernon's *Daily Argus* reported that all the houses in Lawrence Park (as it was then called) were soon to be occupied.[iii]

Lawrence hired architect William Bates to subdivide the farm, lay out streets, and design the first speculative houses. Bates had been one of the chief architects of Tuxedo Park's cottages. He approached Lawrence Park as Tuxedo Park on a smaller scale. Although the density of Lawrence Park was much greater than that of Tuxedo, Bates's design alleviated the sense of crowding by leaving in place trees, streams, and outcroppings. His early houses were more Shingle in style, but within a few years they evolved into Tudor with its half-timbering.[iv]

At first an artist's colony, Lawrence Park grew rapidly, and by 1898 it was incorporated within the village of Bronxville. Growth inspired Lawrence to call on Bates to construct rental apartments near the commercial center. Tudor was chosen for the style, echoing that of the houses in Lawrence Park. Bates and

Lawrence established Tudor as the style in Bronxville, one that continued after Bates's death in 1922.

Foremost among the talented architects who continued the style was Lewis Bowman. He began his career with McKim, Mead & White where he worked the summers of 1911–13, but, unhappy with the work there, he returned to his native Westchester and joined a small real estate and construction firm in Mount Vernon called Gramatan Homes. Through this association Bowman became acquainted with the area's best craftsmen. He established his own practice in 1918. By 1920, after he had designed several houses in succession in Bronxville, his reputation spread, and he was soon designing houses for some of Wall Street's prominent moneymen in the aptly named "stockbroker Tudor" style. Bowman's architectural roots were in Cotswold, England, as were many

LEFT: *Bolton Gardens. In 1920 the twenty-two attached houses in Bolton Gardens faced a quadrangle set well back from the road. Four years later another ten units, mostly fronting the road, were added.*

RIGHT AND CENTER: *Merestone Terrace. Architect Penrose Stout designed the community houses of broken stone and half-timber in 1924. Although the eleven units resemble a rambling English country house, they are constructed in a shallow L-shape on a small lot near a busy road.*

of the designs of the English architect Sir Edwin Lutyens, who influenced him greatly. Bowman's work during the 1920s gave the village some of its most dramatic houses, which had the added contemporary features of luxury and order in demand by the newly successful. To drive through Bronxville today is to experience the romance and beauty of picturesque houses in a setting that seems made for them.

The four houses that follow illustrate Bowman's work.

Sullivan House

BRONXVILLE, NEW YORK

Lewis Bowman, 1920s

THE ELM ROCK ESTATES SECTION OF BRONXVILLE
was subdivided in about 1920. Lots were a half to a
full acre or more—relatively large for Bronxville—
allowing for rather substantial houses. During the
1920s twelve houses were built in the new division,
eight of them designed by Lewis Bowman. The
natural beauty of the hilly terrain with huge boulders
and outcroppings and large stands of old trees
appealed to Bowman so much that he and his wife
built their own home there in 1920.

Bowman designed this house for Frederick K.
Shaff, chairman of Combustion Engineering Super
Heating. The house is set toward the rear of the site,
allowing the preservation of many of the old trees
and a large front lawn.

ABOVE AND RIGHT: *The rear of the house shows Bowman's attention to detail there as well as on the street façade.[v] A curved stone footbridge leads to a covered terrace and the rear of the house.*

Elm Rock is dominated by picturesque but difficult sites. The terrain was ideally suited for Bowman's skills. For this house Bowman created an irregular floor plan with a zigzag footprint following the ravine and the steep hillside behind it while preserving the many overarching beautiful trees. His irregular plans combined with irregular massing allow his houses to seem larger than they actually are. The plans also gave each house an individuality.[vi] Most of the Bowman houses in the neighborhood have four main bedrooms, making them a manageable size and highly usable today.[vii]

Rappaport House
BRONXVILLE, NEW YORK
Lewis Bowman, 1921

FEW HOUSES BETTER EXHIBIT BOWMAN TRADEMARKS than this house in Elm Rock Estates. Stone quarried from the site is lavishly used. Irregular massing, complex chimneys, textured slate roof, and leaded glass windows were part of the Bowman vocabulary. And yet, the house lacks the showiness that became associated with the era's mansions along the Hudson or on Long Island. Rather, Bowman's extravagance appears more subtly in the architectural details that speak of tradition and craftsmanship.

As with many Bowman houses, this one shows the influence of British architect Edwin Lutyens, many of whose designs were drawn from the simplicity of the English Cotswold style. Like Lutyens residences, the lines are simple and without roof overhangs.

LEFT: *The entry hall is reminiscent of a Jacobean courtyard, with a slate floor and stone on one wall.*[viii] *Exposed structural timbers on other walls and the ceiling contribute to the effect.*

ABOVE: *Extensive oak paneling, a limestone fireplace, and the beamed ceiling in the living room are classic features of Bowman interiors. English pieces furnished the room.*

The sunroom, with its arched leaded-glass windows, overlook the house's natural setting. The rough stone of the walls is masterfully designed to reflect the surrounding rocky landscape.

Bowman lived in this house until financial reverses during the Depression forced him to sell it and move into his studio.[ix] His practice had flourished in the Roaring Twenties, but even before the crash of October 1929, it was undermined when his assistant, Robert Scannell, started his own local practice, hoping to secure some of the commissions for houses for the wealthy elite. When the crash struck, Bowman was unable to sell the several speculative houses he was just finishing. Other legal misfortunes befell him, and he was forced to move into his studio with his family. Although he continued to practice, he never fully recovered his former success. After World War II, the demand for Tudor mansions evaporated. He lived in a Greenwich Village apartment in the mid-1960s and died in 1970, leaving a legacy of picturesque houses built within about a decade. Today, their existence has returned his reputation to its former prominence.[x]

Gogel House

BRONXVILLE, NEW YORK

Lewis Bowman, 1926

LEWIS BOWMAN'S MASTERY OF HIS BUILDING MATERIALS is evident in this Tudor house of gables and bays with hexagonally paned windows. The gables illustrate his creativity in using the regularity of brick in contrast with rough stonework and the irregularity of the roof's slate tiles. The interplay of several patterns creates a highly textured surface. The ornately carved bargeboards, pendants, and brackets create deep shadows that also animate the surface.[xi]

Shaffer House

BRONXVILLE, NEW YORK

Lewis Bowman, 1928

DURING THE 1920S, CORNELL-EDUCATED LEWIS Bowman was one of the most respected domestic architects in the country. Of his thirty-eight designs published in that decade, twenty-five were built in Bronxville, all in some way Tudor in style. His designs show the influence of Edwin Lutyens, who, with C. F. A. Voysey and Baillie Scott, were for Americans the leaders of British domestic architecture. Lutyens's influence on Bowman's designs can be seen in his overscaled chimney clusters, grouped and intersecting gables, and undulating lines.[xii]

This house, designed by Lewis Bowman in 1928, is a particularly handsome design of the English half-timber style. A cluster of five chimneys punctuates the heavy slate roof whose ridge rises slightly at each end, creating the impression that the house is centuries old and has settled with age.

Bowman and his contemporaries were masterful in their use of stucco, timbers, stone, brick, and slate. Today, Bowman's houses endure because of their fine craftsmanship and because they succeed in combining a design that evokes the past with a timelessness that accommodates the enjoyment of a comfortable contemporary life.

UPPER LEFT: *Detail of a finial and the fine interior woodwork that was a trademark of Bowman's work.*

LOWER LEFT: *The hallway steps and a coved ceiling lead to the living room.*

FACING PAGE: *The two-story living room with its open balcony is reminiscent of the medieval great hall.*

ABOVE: *The living room illustrates characteristic elements of a Bowman interior—the oak paneling, arched doorways, and substantial stone fireplace surround. The carved beams give the room a particularly dramatic effect.*

RIGHT: *The house was built for executive Royal B. Mudge. Sited in a shallow valley, it is protected from the street by low stone walls. The siting and lush plantings give the house the appearance of always having been there. Bowman himself characterized the style of the house as Picturesque.*

Mount Vernon

MOUNT VERNON, WHICH BORDERS BRONXVILLE TO the south, was developed in 1850 as a working- and middle-class community. Unlike Bronxville, with its curving streets, Mount Vernon was laid out on a grid plan of straight streets. John Stevens, who worked diligently to improve the condition of the working class in New York City by making a property-holding class out of rent payers, created the development. Mount Vernon was incorporated as a city by 1892. The railroad cut through the city, dividing it into a north and south side. Although the houses of Mount Vernon claim no one architectural style, the north side has many Tudor houses. Developed in the 1920s and 1930s, this section of Mount Vernon gives evidence of Tudor's popularity. Here the influence of the Arts and Crafts movement can also be seen in more modest houses with the white plaster walls and stone or brick trim made popular by the English Arts and Crafts architecture of Voysey and Baillie Scott.

*These streetscapes display the
variety of Tudor houses in
Mount Vernon's hilly and
wooded terrain.*

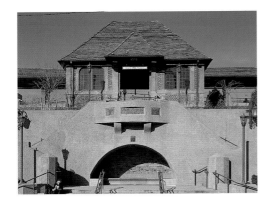

The train station entrance.

Forest Hills Gardens

FOREST HILLS WAS DEVELOPED IN 1909 BY THE Russell Sage Foundation as the first garden city in America. A Progressive-era organization, the foundation was dedicated to providing decent schools and housing for the less well off. The foundation purchased a hundred acres of Queensborough farmland, thirteen minutes by rail from Manhattan, with the intention of providing housing for moderate income and middle-class commuters as an alternative to cramped city flats. Frederick Law Olmsted Jr., son of the great landscape designer, served as Forest Hills' planner and landscape designer, and Grosvenor Atterbury was its architect.

They organized their plan around picturesque Station Square, which is dominated by a clock tower and lined with arcaded shops. Leaving the plaza to reach the residential neighborhoods, one passes under a covered bridge.

Atterbury developed a new method of construction for the main buildings using precast concrete slabs molded on the construction site. This method was intended to ensure permanence and low maintenance for the buildings. To give an old English village appearance to the square, the slabs were faced with bricks, pebbles, and crushed terra-cotta tile arranged in panels with exposed bands of concrete stained to resemble half-timbering. The jerkinhead roofs and dormers on most of the buildings were as much German as English. This influence, however, disappeared after 1914.[xiii]

Closest to the station are semi-detached houses and row houses, while single-family residences are farther away on curving streets forming their own enclaves. Hampstead Garden suburb in London, also planned in 1909 and intended to relieve urban living conditions, had much in common with Forest Hills. Raymond Unwin, Hampstead's planner, advocated groups of double houses arranged around shared greens in U-shape or crescents with the houses set well back from gently curving streets.[xiv]

LEFT: *A row of Tudor Style apartment buildings line this street in Forest Hills.*

ABOVE: *The West Side Tennis Club, built in 1914 in a style that is picturesque Tudor, the dominant style of Forest Hills. The club was long the home of the U.S. Open Tennis Tournament.*

Styles other than Tudor were built in Forest Hills, but most architects tended to follow Atterbury's preference for picturesque old English designs, which became the predominant architecture of the community.

Single-family residences are set well back from the tree-lined streets, allowing ample sidewalks as well as expanses of green lawns, shrubbery, and flowers. Only the boulevards giving access into and out of the suburb are straight. Neighborhood streets, branching off from them, curve to form individual enclaves.

Forest Hills Gardens, with its larger houses, was simply too good and too convenient to Manhattan to remain a moderate-income suburb. As real estate values rose, upper-middle class city-dwellers began to displace people of more moderate means until it became the exclusive community it is today. The winding streets are privately owned and maintained by an association of Forest Hills homeowners. Street parking is by permit only. The Russell Sage Foundation sold its property rights to the association in 1922.

Teaneck, New Jersey

MANY TOWNS IN NEW JERSEY SERVE AS NEW YORK City suburbs. Teaneck is just across the George Washington Bridge from the upper reaches of Manhattan. Many residents commute to the city daily.

Conventional Tudor houses are prevalent in Teaneck's Winthrop and Standish Road Historic Districts. Each house is unique, but they share the prominent steep gable, the stone, brick, or stucco materials, and the distinctive chimneys of the Tudor style.

Tudor Revival in Teaneck's
Winthrop and Standish Road
Historic District

BLANTYRE CASTLE

WESTCHESTER TRUMPS ALL OTHER AREAS FOR THE NUMBER OF ITS TUDOR HOUSES. HOWEVER, the East Coast has an abundant number outside of that county and further away from New York City. Lenox, Massachusetts is about three hours from New York City. In the 1890s Scotsman Robert Paterson, a successful merchant, had occasion to visit a friend there. At the time, because of its many great estates, the community had come to be known as "the queen of inland resorts." Paterson was so taken with the area and its elegant way of life that he decided he wanted to spend summers in Lenox with his family.

He acquired 220 acres of Lenox property and began building a spectacular residence, indeed a castle, modeled after his wife's ancestral home in Lanarkshire, Scotland. Construction began in 1901 at times employing as many as 300 people. In addition to the main house, there were seven outbuildings, including an icehouse, stables for sixteen horses, a carriage house, and extensive greenhouses.

The Paterson family used the house every summer and entertained frequently, as was the fashion in the days of the Gilded Age. Each party became more lavish than the one before with opulent dinner dances and guests at garden parties wandering the grounds to the strains of musicians imported from New York.

The introduction of the income tax twenty years later brought the era to an end, its lifestyle never to be repeated. Over the next sixty years, Blantyre went through several changes in ownership, including a destructive period in the 1970s. In 1980 Jack and Jane Fitzpatrick bought the property and, after a year of extensive renovation, restored it to its original elegance as a beautiful country house estate. In 2000 ownership of Blantyre passed to their daughter Ann Fitzpatrick Brown, who further perfected the estate.

ABOVE AND FACING PAGE: *The dramatic circular drive travels alongside the great lawn of the estate, leading to a covered entranceway.*

ABOVE: *Paterson's concept for the estate was a castle of "feudal architectural features." Replete with turrets and gargoyles, the house is an eclectic blend of half timbering, clustered chimneys, and leaded glass windows of the Tudor style.*

FACING PAGE: *A view of the drive from the covered entranceway.*

FACING PAGE: *The music room is appropriately furnished with various musical instruments— an 1860 grand piano, a harp, a mandolin, and a violoncello (as seen above). A signed Tiffany lamp, a 1760 Italian china cabinet, a Dutch marquetry desk and china cabinet, Persian rugs, and oil and water color paintings contribute to the room's old world ambiance. Originally, the most important painting in the music room was of Bismarck, painted by Lembach. It has been replaced by one of Henry Clive, painted by John Opie.*

FACING PAGE: *The Patersons
furnished the main house with
antiques bought in England.
Their extensive art collection
supplied many of the house's
paintings. The Fitzpatricks
replaced the Patersons' long-
since-dispersed furnishings
with an eclectic mix of
period pieces, including the*

*Chinese Export bowls and
vases seen on the table and mantel
(as seen above). Intricately
carved fireplace surrounds of
burnished wood and parged
ceilings from the time when the
house was built are emblematic
of the Tudor style.*

The paneled dining room is furnished with period pieces, an antique rug, and oil paintings.

ABOVE: *Like the Great Hall of the Tudor period, which was used for family living rather than just as a circulation space, the grand staircase ascends from the house's main parlor.*

FACING PAGE: *During the day leaded and stained glass windows open to views of the great lawn and the Berkshire mountains beyond. At night they become glowing lanterns.*

PHILADELPHIA SUBURBS

THE FIELDSTONE COTSWOLD-STYLE TUDOR HOUSE IS A UNIQUE CHARACTERISTIC OF THE SUBURBS in and around Philadelphia. Tudor houses are found wherever suburbs grew between the turn of the century and into the 1930s. Whether in Bronxville, Shaker Heights, or Lake Forest the character of such houses is sufficiently similar that identifying their locale is difficult. However, some regional variations do exist. The Philadelphia area's Cotswold houses are an example of a distinct regional Tudor type.[i]

The suburb of Chestnut Hill, one of the region's most beautiful, contains a wealth of such dwellings. That so coherent an architecture developed is due to a combination of elements. Chestnut Hill is set in the Wissahickon Valley in the heart of the gray ledge stone deposits that have been used in Philadelphia construction from its earliest days. Known as Wissahickon schist, the stone is easily quarried and plentiful. The city was settled by middle-class Quakers, unpretentious people who valued simplicity. They, along with Germanic groups, came from regions with long traditions of stone building. In William Penn's colony they found material to match their talents. Over the decades, Quaker families tended to remain in place, passing their traditions from one generation to the next. Thus, Philadelphia continued to be a conservative community attuned to its English heritage.

In addition to the ubiquitous stone and the community's interest in English architectural developments, the presence of one particular real estate developer, Dr. George Woodward, contributed greatly to the character of Chestnut Hill and as a result to that of many suburbs surrounding Philadelphia.

TOP: *Although American Craftsman-like porches front these early Woodward houses, overall they have an English look. They are alike in that all are the same height and have English gables. They are, however, faced in different materials, some in brick, some in stucco, some in stone, and here and there some half-timbering.*

BOTTOM: *Facing the double houses of Benezet Street are a mix of quadruple, single, and double houses.*

George Woodward Developments

CHESTNUT HILL, PENNSYLVANIA

EARLY IN THE TWENTIETH CENTURY GEORGE Woodward, with his wife Gertrude, daughter of Henry Howard Houston, who had initiated Chestnut Hill's development, began constructing a series of influential housing complexes that would create an identifiable architectural look in the community. Influenced by the Arts and Crafts movement, English town planning, and frequent trips to Europe, Woodward called principally on Philadelphia architects Herman Duhring (1874–1953), Edmund Gilchrist (1880–1953), and Robert R. McGoodwin (1886–1967) to design the simple lines of these English stone structures that drew on the late-medieval cottages of the Cotswolds.

Cotswold houses were built of one material with no overhanging eaves and no half-timbering. Casement windows were set flush with the walls, as were dormers. Chimneys were block-like rather than the elaborately carved clusters of other Tudor styles. Window and door surrounds were either of the same fieldstone or of pale limestone. Corners were articulated with larger blocks of fieldstone rather than limestone quoins. The general restraint of the style and its elegant simplicity were well suited to the Quaker heritage of Philadelphia, and to the sensibilities of Dr. George Woodward.

Wissahickon schist is similar to the stone of the Cotswold hills of England, both being soft when quarried and hardening when exposed to air. Thus it

was logical that Woodward was drawn to a style that featured a stone so available in Chestnut Hills. Nearly all of the Woodward houses designed by his favorites—McGoodwin, Duhring, and Gilchrist—were in the Cotswold style.

As Gavin Townsend states, "The combination of locally available stone, a community attuned to developments in England, and the presence of George Woodward proved to be unique." [ii] The Cotswold style remains the Philadelphia area's regional variation of Tudor revival.

George Woodward initiated his first building campaign in 1910. He commissioned the architectural firm of Duhring Okie and Ziegler to design houses intended for workers. On Benezet Street they created

ABOVE: *Three Woodward houses front a center garden.*

rows of double houses on one side of the street and a mix of quadruple, single, and double houses on the other, a design inspired by English garden city planning for such developments as Letchworth and Hampstead Garden suburb. Eventually, Woodward commissioned more than 160 houses, almost all in the Cotswold style. Many other builders saw its attractions and its suitability to the region. Woodward's Cotswold houses set the standard for future development in and around Philadelphia.

House in Mount Airy

MOUNT AIRY, PENNSYLVANIA

Mellor, Meigs & Howe, Architects, 1916

AS THE HOUSES IN THIS CHAPTER SHOW, THE MOST
cohesive and distinctive of the regional schools
of architecture flourished in the Philadelphia area.
The noted architectural firm of Mellor, Miegs &
Howe designed many of the area's most beautiful
country houses in the suburbs and countryside
near Philadelphia. These socially well-connected
gentlemen designers were Anglophile traditionalists
who perpetuated the distinctive Philadelphia architecture, drawing on the vernacular building traditions
of rural England as well as the simple buildings of
rural Pennsylvania. In doing so, they followed the
example of English Arts and Crafts masters C. F. A.
Voysey, M. H. Baillie Scott, and Edwin Lutyens in the
sensitive handling of their materials—Wissahickon
schist, rustic brick, and stucco. They were supported
in their romantic pastoral designs by the conservatism
of the city's patrons who insisted on identifying with
their ancestors.[iii]

This house was built the year Howe joined
Mellor and Meigs. It personifies the farm cottage
nestled into the landscape like a secluded Cotswold
village. It shows the advancing and receding gable
masses and the texture of the mellow stone that
characterized their early work.

*This 1916 house is in Chestnut
Hill's nearby suburb of
Mount Airy. Designed by the
architectural firm of Mellor,
Meigs & Howe, who designed
many beautiful houses in the
mellow stone of the Philadelphia
area, it is identified as Arts
and Crafts by the owner.*

*However, it is difficult to
differentiate it from Cotswold
for it shares the simplicity
of line and other elements
of Cotswold style. The interior's
handcrafted woodwork and
hand-hewn beams reflect the
Arts and Crafts movement's
emphasis on handicraft.*

The main house is a two-story structure with a trio of clustered chimneys in characteristic Tudor style. To the left is the kitchen attachment.

Peter Lapham Complex

CHESTNUT HILL, PENNSYLVANIA

THIS COMPLEX OF BUILDINGS WAS ASSEMBLED BETWEEN 1926 and 1928. It consists of two types of structures built in different countries during different periods of time and then moved to the present location. The brick dwelling was a sixteenth-century English cottage. The outbuildings are also from the original site. While it is not certain that all of the bricks were brought from England, much of the material, such as the timbers, limestone roof tiles, and some windows, were imported from the original buildings.

Robert McGoodwin assembled the complex of buildings during the period of 1926 to 1928. He created a stone addition of Chestnut Hill's Wissahickon schist at the time. That its architecture is very much like the Cotswold style of other houses in the Philadelphia region is not surprising. McGoodwin was one of George Woodward's architects. Woodward was responsible for promoting the Philadelphia area's unique regional Tudor architecture—the stone Cotswold style.

FACING PAGE: *The main house with a chimney that was added.*

RIGHT: *A detail of a downspout. The leaded glass windows are characteristic of the Tudor style.*

BELOW: *The garage roof is covered with limestone tiles, which were imported from the original structure.*

ABOVE: *Ample leaded glass casement windows line the living room. Their surrounds are of oak, as are the ceiling timbers.*

BELOW: *A connection between the kitchen and the main house was needed, so the conservatory was constructed, connecting the cottage to the main house kitchen.*

FACING PAGE: *The kitchen ceiling is beamed with Tudor-style timbers and leaded casementscarry out the design.*

FACING PAGE: *A converted garage bed-room. The ceiling's complex timbering is made all the more dramatic by light from a leaded glass window in the dormer. The walls are of Wissahickon schist.*

RIGHT: *The bath is also part of the garage conversion.*

BELOW: *Two upstairs bedrooms in the cottage.*

ABOVE: *The driveway of the complex is lined with trees among which nestle the various structures—main house, cottage, and garage.*

RIGHT: *Each of the outbuildings is constructed in the style of the main house, giving the complex a coherence and charm to which the newer stone dwelling fits as though it was a natural addition from successive generations.*

FACING PAGE: *Another farm building that had been used as a sheep shed.*

THE MIDWEST

IN THE EARLY YEARS OF THEIR CAREERS—THE MID-1890s—MANY OF THE ARCHITECTS WHO CAME to be associated with the Prairie school of architecture, including Frank Lloyd Wright, designed houses based on traditional styles such as Tudor. But with the development of the Prairie style, its vocabulary came to be incorporated in many Tudor designs, creating a regional variation that featured the horizontal features of the wide overhangs associated with Prairie style.

In 1893, Chicago's World's Columbian Exposition with its famous sparkling white, neoclassical buildings created a renewed interest in Colonial and Georgian styles. Less well known was the presence of "Victoria House," the headquarters of the Royal British Commission to the fair. Unlike the completely half-timbered British buildings of the 1876 Centennial, which had awakened an interest in medieval architecture, this structure confined its half-timbering to the second floor. Bands of brick and terra-cotta faced the lower story and awnings fluttered in the breeze. Although the building appeared as much Victorian as Tudor, a guidebook to the exposition termed it Elizabethan in style and "a typical example of the half-timbered manor house of the Tudor period."[i] The building appears to have had an influence on at least one of Wright's colleagues, Robert Closson Spencer Jr., Wright's friend and office-mate in the Shiller building in downtown Chicago. Spencer designed many Tudor houses, some archaeologically correct versions, others that merged Prairie school elements. Spencer may have influenced Wright in his design of the clearly Tudor Nathan Moore House in Oak Park.[ii]

Wright's Moore House was a stylized version of Tudor. The same year that he built that house, he remodeled another Oak Park residence employing a steep, half-timbered gable. Also in 1895, he built a pair of townhouses minus the half-timbering but with Tudor-Gothic gables and details that evoked late medieval architecture.[iii]

Wright continued to abstract and to simplify Tudor elements, particularly half-timbering, until their source was no longer obvious. Two of his earliest Prairie houses, the Harley Bradley and Warren Hickox houses in Kankakee (1900), have gables and half-timbering. Gavin Townsend mentions that the Japanese pavilion at the 1893 Exposition, Ho-o-den, may have inspired the half-timbered gables with overhanging eaves. However, unlike the Japanese pavilion whose timbers extend the full height of the house, those of the Hickox House are confined to the gable in an English manner.[iv] That Wright was interested in this Tudor element is evident in the half-timbering between the casement windows of the otherwise Prairie stone Ward Willets house of 1902. It can be seen as the culmination of a seven-year progression of abstracting that had begun with the Moore House.

The fusion of Prairie with Tudor developed a regional version of the Tudor style. However, it lasted only until World War I when there was a return to the more accurate and conservative Tudor designs. Wright's avant-garde Prairie houses were expensive to build. Those who commissioned them tended to be upper middle class. But as such clients traveled more often abroad or to the East Coast, they, and especially their wives, were influenced by what they saw. What they wanted were houses that would stand as monuments to their status in life. Their architectural confidence was shaken by the new, low-slung structures designed by Wright and his confreres of the Midwest. When they commissioned a Tudor house, they wanted the Tudor Revival houses of the East Coast or, indeed, of England, with expensive materials and excellent craftsmanship.

When Wright left the Chicago area, the Prairie style appears to have departed with him. In the years following the war, a new conservatism developed in midwestern architecture.[v] After the war, especially in the 1920s and 1930s, Tudor houses sprang up in the wealthy suburbs of Chicago just as they did elsewhere throughout the country. Chicago's postwar Tudor houses were little different from those in the suburbs of New York, Detroit, Houston, or San Francisco.

Nathan Moore House

OAK PARK, ILLINOIS

Frank Lloyd Wright, 1895–1923

IN 1895 FRANK LLOYD WRIGHT'S FRIEND AND NEIGHBOR, Nathan Moore, came to him with a commission to design an expensive residence in the English Tudor style. Wright, who rejected historicist references as unsuited to the life of modern families, nevertheless agreed. He was just starting out on his own; he had a growing family. So, Tudor it was, but Wright put his own and stamp on the style. His design featured steeply pitched gables with half-timbering, massive medieval chimneys, and diamond-pane casement windows but in a somewhat abstract form. The gables were steeper, the chimney more monolithic than any medieval version, the patterning of the half-timbering more cleanly geometric than traditional half-timbering.

On Christmas Day, 1922, the house caught fire.
Although it was rumored that the original construction
had bankrupted Moore, he commissioned Wright to
design plans for its reconstruction. Wright retained
the walls of thin Roman brick, but above them he
erected roofs that were even taller and more acutely
pointed than those of the original house. Not above a
certain eclecticism, on the first floor Wright included
a bay with Gothic windows. Decorative trim around
the second-floor terrace hints at the future designs of
Wright's Japanese and California years.[vi]

Broad Lea

LAKE FOREST, ILLINOIS

Howard Van Doren Shaw, 1898

THIS HOUSE IS ONE OF HOWARD VAN DOREN SHAW'S earliest in Lake Forest. In 1894 at the age of 23, after working two or three years in the office of William Le Baron Jenney, a firm known for its tall building designs, Shaw established his own practice, working out of his father's house in Chicago. Early in his career Shaw shared an interest with his Prairie school contemporaries in the English Arts and Crafts architecture of Voysey and Baillie Scott. Indeed, he might have joined the Prairie school. However, with a few commissions from wealthy meatpacking and steel

industrialists for grand Tudor houses, he was soon established as architect to the elite.

In 1898 he built his own country house, Ragdale, in Lake Forest. Money and connections soon brought him commissions such as Broad Lea, built not long after his own, for a prominent physician, Dr. Nathan Smith Davis Jr., son of one of the founders of Northwestern University.

Although the house is described in the town's Historic Resources Survey as English Cottage, his original design had eclectic elements of the Colonial

Revival and the Shingle Style. The first and second floors were shingled. Twin gables and brick chimneys with decorative corbeling at the top on either end were also part of the design.

Subsequently, the north side of the house was remodeled. Instead of the original shingles, the first story is now sheathed in brick. A second-story half-timbered bay projects from the main block of the house. Supported on piers, the bay shelters the recessed entrance. On the second story a double-hung window has been added to the original fenestration.

Although little information is available about the date or the architect who carried out the remodeling, the broad, low eaves that were added create horizontality and suggest the influence of the Prairie school that the original house lacked.

By 1905 Shaw was known as one of the leading country house architects in America. He also established a reputation for his industrial, commercial, and institutional work. He belonged to many social clubs and organizations. In 1926 he was awarded the American Institute of Architects' Gold Medal.

Derwen Mawr

LAKE FOREST, ILLINOIS

David Adler & Robert Work, 1922

THE FIRM OF ADLER AND WORK DESIGNED DERWEN MAWR. Adler (1882–1949), a noted architect whose work is significant to the history and development of Lake Forest, has been described as the last of the great eclectic architects. He designed at least fifty houses in a range of styles that included Italian Renaissance villas, French chateaux, and Georgian and American Colonial. Most of his country houses and country clubs were built on Chicago's North Shore, particularly in Lake Forest, although some of his most important work is found in suburbs from coast to coast and in Hawaii.

An 1894 Princeton graduate, Adler continued his studies at the Ecole des Beaux Arts in Paris, but did not receive certification because he failed to complete the work. After leaving, he traveled widely in Europe, concentrating on style and detail. The technical and structural aspects of architecture never really interested him. In 1911, when he returned to Chicago, he and an Ecole friend, Henry C. Dangler, went to work for Howard Van Doren Shaw. Dangler soon left to open his own office and Adler joined him not long after. The two worked together until Dangler's death in 1917. Adler did not have an Illinois license but Dangler did, so his name was used for building permit purposes. Adler was finally granted a license in recognition of demonstration of skill in 1928.

This house was built for Owen Barton Jones, a man of many interests and a world traveler. He hired Adler to design the original east section in 1922. In 1932 Jones had the house enlarged. Wolcott & Work completed the west wing and some of the outbuildings on the estate.

Glimpses of the twenty-eight-room Flemish bond mansion can be seen through an orchard as the house is approached from a long, curving drive. The entrance, slightly recessed behind two thin columns that support a crenelated bay on the second story, is in the center of the three prominent gable ends. Rising above the slate roof are several multivent chimneys.

ABOVE: *Walcott & Work adapted ideas and details from an Elizabethan manor house in Sutton Courtenay, Berkshire, England, that was owned by a friend of Owen Barton Jones. Elaborately carved bargeboards of a floral motif trim the gable ends in typical sixteenth-century style.*

OPPOSITE: *The crenelated bay rises above the entrance porte cochere. Originally thirty-three acres of rolling terrain with groves, gardens, terraces, and an orchard of flowering fruit trees, portions of the estate have been donated for a nature preserve.*[vii]

West View Farms

LAKE FOREST, ILLINOIS

Howard Van Doren Shaw, 1924–25

BY THE TIME HOWARD VAN DOREN SHAW DESIGNED
West View Farms he had been practicing for more than
twenty-five years, having started his own practice in
1895 at the age of 24. By 1905 he was known as one of
the leading country house architects in America.

His designs show the strong influence of British
architect Edwin Luytens, master of the vernacular
stone house amd Shaw's favorite architect.[viii] The evo-
lution of his work can be seen by comparing his early
house, Broad Lea (pages 116–117), with its eclectic
combination of Colonial Revival and Shingle Style elements to this Cotswold style residence with its prominent intersecting gables, block chimneys, simple lines,
and unadorned walls all of one material—brick.

West View Farms was built in 1924–25 for Robert
P. Lamont, Secretary of Commerce for the Hoover
administration. Constructed of brick, with limestone
and wood trim, the influence of Edwin Lutyens'
vernacular designs is evident.

The arched entrance hall (above left), oak-paneled corridor (above right), and living room (below left) show the attention to detail and craftsmanship that was characteristic of Shaw's work. Few alterations have been made to the historic fabric of the residence. In 1993, it was carefully rehabilitated and restored.

A view of the gardens (far right) from a bay with floor-to-ceiling windows.

Rear views of the house. Although it is unknown what the grounds looked like just after the house was built, old photographs indicate that the landscaping was informal, with hardwoods planted on a gently sloping lawn. Originally 102 acres, the estate is now a little over seven acres.

*The wavy pattern of the shingles
and their rounded moulding
over the eaves gives the residence
its rustic look of thatching.
The chimney is made to look like
a tower also offering housing
for birds.*

Smith Pirie House

LAKE FOREST, ILLINOIS

Hart & Shape, 1929

THE BRITISH REVIVAL OF VERNACULAR COTTAGES
that looked much like those of sixteenth-century
Tudor England were built during the seventeenth
and eighteenth centuries in Britain. Designed to
look quaint and picturesque, many employed the
thatching and half-timbering of yeoman cottages. By
the late nineteenth century, Tudor Revival began
in America. As in England its forms were based on the
vernacular cottages and manor houses of sixteenth-
and seventeenth-century England.

The thatched cottage had a particular romantic
appeal. Perhaps that is why Franklin Smith chose this
version of a yeoman cottage as a wedding gift to his
daughter Daisiana and John T. Pirie Jr., the son of one
of the founders of the Chicago department store,
Carson Pirie Scott.

FAR LEFT: *Above the entrance a stair runs up the side of the house leading to a balcony and a second-story entrance.*

LEFT: *The muntined door has leaded glass and a flat Tudor arch.*

The original thatch of yeoman cottages was laid on a steeply pitched roof so that the rain would easily run off. Unfortunately, in North America's colder climate, snow was not so easily shed. Also, thatch was susceptible to fire. Various retardants were unsuccessfully experimented with. One was a method that would cause the thatch not to "flame to any extent" but rather to "sizzle very slowly so that it could be easily extinguished."[ix] By the time the Smith-Pirie house was built, thatch had been abandoned, undoubtedly also having something to do with insurance rates, if not the safety of the owners themselves. But a substitute was found.

A method had been developed to steam cedar shingles in order to bend them over the furred edges of the roof, laying them in uneven rows to simulate thatch. The shingled brow of the roof overhangs the windows and balcony door of the second story and curves over rounded gables and dormers. The thatched-shingle roof became one of the most popular coverings between 1910 and 1925 in spite of the fact that it was twice as expensive as a normal shingle roof, in fact about as much as slate.[x] But then, slate would not have been as romantic a choice.

Strips of casement windows emphasize the horizontality of the dwelling. Walls are stuccoed and the entrance is enlivened by stonework. In 1964, new owners acquired the house and restored it to its original appearance.

ABOVE: *The living room is entered through a flat Tudor-arched doorway.*

FACING PAGE: *The sunroom wing to the right of the main block of the house is flooded with light and beamed in the Tudor manner.*

This house and the house on page 137 are two examples of Tudor-style model houses in Shaker Village. One of the innovative promotional devices used by the Van Sweringens was the construction of model houses to demonstrate what a client might expect in Shaker Village. Although real estate agents scoffed at the method, it is said 40,000 people toured the models and all sixteen of the houses are still standing.

Shaker Heights

SHAKER HEIGHTS, OHIO

THE 1,360 ACRES OF WOODS, ORCHARDS, LAKES, AND farmland of the North Union Shaker settlement was the nucleus of the land developed as Shaker Village, later Shaker Heights.[xi]

Although the 1822 Shaker settlement prospered and attracted many new members, the dream of the Shakers for a utopian religious community of farmers, craftsmen, and artisans faded with the booming industrial rise of Cleveland in the last quarter of the nineteenth century. Membership steadily declined until only twenty-seven members remained, and in 1889 the elders decided to sell their land holdings and relocate.

In 1905 Oris Paxton and his brother Mantis James Van Sweringen acquired a portion of the land with the intention of developing a residential community. Experience had taught them that a transportation system was needed to get people living in Cleveland to commute to the development. Without it the trip took the better part of the afternoon. In 1920 they bought an existing railroad line from the New York Central and extended it into Shaker Village. With its completion in 1920, successful development, previously shaky, was assured. From a community of 200

in 1911, it grew to 1,600 in 1920, and 18,000 in 1930. In the peak building year, 1925, some 500 building permits were issued, and by 1931 it officially became the City of Shaker Heights.[xii]

Development of Shaker Village followed the Garden City idea of small districts subdivided while preserving land to serve as green space and parks. The planners added a system of broad, elliptical boulevards with green medians to the road system that already existed. Building setbacks were strictly enforced, creating spacious lawns with sycamores, elms, and maples. Inherited from the Shakers were two man-made lakes to which the developers added another two smaller ones.

The Van Sweringen Company's promotional brochure, *Peaceful Shaker Village*, reflected the mood of romanticism in the 1920s. For those Americans who had never traveled abroad, films brought to them French chateaux, Gothic cathedrals, and, of course, Tudor manor houses of the English countryside. Wealthy Americans created the Country House movement. The Shaker Heights real estate development with its varying lot size made it possible for those less wealthy as well.

The houses of Shaker Heights could be built for
a wide range of prices, depending on the street and
the lot size. But in order to insure uniformity of value
and to provide for varying degrees of financial status,
uniformity of lot sizes within each district was carefully regulated. A 1923 brochure for Shaker Village
showed houses of all classes and styles already built,
including Tudor and Cotswold.

18302

Van Sweringen Mansion

SHAKER HEIGHTS, OHIO

Original design by H. T. Jeffries, remodeled by Phillip Small and Charles B. Rowley, 1924

THE VAN SWERINGEN BROTHERS BUILT AN IMPRESSIVE
English Tudor mansion on South Park Boulevard.
It was intended not so much as a residence for them-
selves as a symbol to residents and prospective buyers
alike of their continuing interest in Shaker Village.
They eventually gave the house to their two unmar-
ried sisters, preferring to live in their suite at the
Terminal Tower or, later, at their country estate at
Daisy Hill.

PREVIOUS PAGE, ABOVE, AND OVERLEAF: *The asymmetrical house, as originally designed by H. T. Jeffries, was rather undistinguished. In 1924, architects Phillip Small and Charles B. Rowley remodeled it into a much more fashionable Tudor Revival mansion. Its steep, all-embracing roof is punctuated by half-timbered gables and dormers. A crenelated tower and beautifully ornamented, clustered chimneys are typical of the Tudor style.*

RIGHT: *In the entry hall, elegant graceful stairs curve upwards over the entrance.*

As seen in the breakfast room (left), the hallway (below), and the dining room (above), handsome paneling is carried throughout the house.

ABOVE: *The dining room with bay windows, decorative panels, and parged ceiling overlooks the gardens.*

The living room (left) and
library (below) contain the
burnished wood paneling seen
throughout the house.

RIGHT: The wine cellar stair is
decorated with charming, painted
medieval characters and cherubs
cavorting among grapevines.

ABOVE: *Detail of a window with herringbone brickwork and half-timbering.*

RIGHT: *The rear entrance tower to the house is constructed of* stone and brick. Half-timbering infill is of bricks and stucco. Paired chimneys are beautifully patterned brick in the Tudor style.

Shaker Heights Residence

SHAKER HEIGHTS, OHIO

Meade and Hamilton, 1923

IN VAN SWERINGEN'S PROMOTIONAL BROCHURE
for Shaker Heights, English style is divided into four
categories: Early English, reflecting the defensive
nature of English society; Tudor; Early Renaissance
(Jacobean); and Garden Style English, an outgrowth
of the English Arts and Crafts movement started
by John Ruskin. While there are variations within the
names, Tudor is the catchall.

Shaker Heights Residence

SHAKER HEIGHTS, OHIO

Bloodgood Tuttle, 1923

THE VAN SWERINGENS EXERCISED STRICT CONTROL over the development of the community. Street and lot size dictated house size. Recommended styles were Colonial, French, and English. Emphasis was on dignity and good taste. A competent architect was required, something that fortunately coincided with the careers of some of the country's outstanding architects working in the popular historic revivalist styles. Among them was Bloodgood Tuttle, who designed this early Tudor Revival house in 1923. Its stonework is particularly fine. Van Sweringen guidelines stressed distinctiveness of design and detail as well as integrity of design. The color of the sash had to be in harmony with the trim. Genuine lead bars were to be used in all glass work instead of zinc, which was deemed flashy and "therefore not in good taste."

The front and rear façade (above) of the house has no half-timbering and is constructed of one material—brick—with simple lines and no over-hanging eaves, features that characterize the Cotswold style. The entrance is embellished with superb stonework. These Tudor houses with their fine masonry clearly meet all of the Van Sweringens' requirements.

ABOVE LEFT: *Large arched doors in this hexagonal entrance hall characterize the handsome architecture.*

The leaded glass arch (opposite) looking into the living room exhibits the fine craftsmanship of the house, as does its wood paneling (below).

ABOVE AND RIGHT: *The fireplace wall of the living room is paneled and the ceiling is beamed in dark wood. Floor to ceiling windows overlook the gardens.*

STAN HYWET HALL

ONE OF THE GRANDEST OF TUDOR REVIVAL ESTATES IN THE UNITED STATES IS THE ONE BUILT IN 1913 by Frank A. Seiberling, founder of the Goodyear Tire and Rubber Company, and his wife Gertrude. The residence they commissioned was a sixty-five-room Tudor Revival mansion, which they called Stan Hywet Hall. For the wealthy, country life was ideal, away from the stresses of urbanization. The estate's 3,000 acres were designed to fill all possible domestic, social, and recreational needs for their family of six children.

Growing up in Akron, Frank Seiberling explored the fields and woods beyond the city. The natural vistas of the Cuyahoga Valley spread before him and affected him deeply. He never forgot them. While the country house filled every recreational need, the land itself was the essential element in defining the estate's character. Boston landscape architect Warren Manning, who had worked for Frederick Law Olmsted and was skilled in the use of native American plants, was engaged by Seiberling to site the house and plan the estate.

Several architects were asked to submit proposals for the design of the house. George B. Post was chosen on the strength of his Tudor-style design. Charles S. Schneider of Cleveland was Post's project architect. In 1912 he accompanied the Seiberlings to Europe to study Tudor manors. Three of the houses they saw particularly influenced them: Ockwells Manor in Berkshire (c. 1450), Compton Wynyates in Warwickshire (c. 1500), and Haddon Hall in Derbyshire (c. 1550). The main entrance is modeled on that of Compton Wynyates. Schneider took his inspiration for the elements of the house from the earlier models they had seen, but changed and updated the details to conform to modern needs. When completed, the house had such modern amenities as central heating, although radiators were secluded from view under window seats, floors, or behind shelves.

A Tudor arch frames the entrance and its English-style enclosed front porch. The motto over the arch, NON NOBIS SOLUM ("not for us alone") well describes the spirit of the house, which was the scene of many parties, charity benefits, and community events. The gable above, now largely hidden by ivy, is ornamented with half-timbering and brick infill. The verge boards are elaborately carved. The crenelated stair tower is to the right.[i]

ABOVE: *The solarium was used as a card and game room. A delightful fountain in the center of the room and leaded, diamond-paned windows are surmounted by an elaborately designed sandalwood ceiling.*

RIGHT: *The round room at the end of the long linenfold hall leads to the music room. The hall's paneling was specially carved for Stan Hywet in the medieval style resembling folds of cloth.*

LEFT: *The two-story Great Hall, the principal room of Tudor houses, was the Seiberlings' living room. Comfortable furniture—easy chairs, sofas, bedroom furniture—was newly made with English antique tables, cabinets, and chairs interspersed.*

ABOVE: *The Seiberlings' daughter Irene's charming bedroom with gabled ceiling and half-timbering, wooden rafters, and leaded glass windows.*

Unlike medieval Tudor houses, most of Stan Hywet Hall's ground floor rooms have large windows that integrate the house with beautiful views of the surrounding gardens, as here in the library.

The music room at the end of the linenfold hallway. Gertrude Seiberling was a trained contralto who knew most of the prominent musicians of the day. Private recitals were often held here. The room was furnished with a concert grand piano, an eighteenth-century harpsichord, and a 2,000-pipe Aeolian organ. The parged ceiling is characteristic of Tudor detail.

ABOVE: *Detail of the intricately carved paneling above the dining room mantelpiece. The house has twenty-three fireplaces.*

RIGHT: *The dining room's ceiling is ornamented with strapwork similar to sixteenth-century motifs.*

The asymmetrical façade has the typical Tudor features of half-timbering, clustered, elaborately carved chimneys, crenelation, and bay windows with leaded lights. The estate accommodated many sporting activities to keep occupied six children, ages seven to twenty-seven—tennis courts, a four-hole golf course, riding trails, a croquet lawn, and a lagoon for canoeing, fishing, swimming, and ice skating. Indoors, the basement housed a swimming pool and a two-story gym where tennis or basketball was played.

In spite of many large and elegant rooms, the house has the intimate atmosphere of family life, albeit a life lived in one of the great houses of the American Country House movement. The house's integrity has been preserved intact for public enjoyment.

CALIFORNIA

TUDOR HOUSES IN CALIFORNIA DID NOT DEVELOP AS A DISTINCT TYPE AS DID THE COTSWOLD cottages of Philadelphia or the Prairie-Tudor houses of the Chicago suburbs. Tudor elements such as half-timbering and windows were often simply added to houses that otherwise were Spanish Colonial or Mediterranean style. One of the most important centers for what could be called a regional Tudor style in southern California was Pasadena.[i] Of the many noted architects who had practices there, none was better known than Henry and Charles Greene (1870–1954 and 1868–1957).

While Frank Lloyd Wright was designing his early houses with Tudor elements in Chicago, the Greene brothers, his contemporaries in California, were working in a style that seemed related visually, but was actually the result of local traditions and the influence of Japanese building techniques.[ii]

The Greenes, who were trained at MIT, began their practice in Pasadena in 1893, building residences in the popular styles desired by clients—Queen Anne or Old English style, Colonial, and Mission styles. At the same time, they were working to develop their own individual architectural character based on their study of wood and a love of natural materials.[iii]

Their early houses combined Tudor elements with those of the Stick Style, Arts and Crafts, and Japanese influences. Thus, half-timbering accompanied houses with projecting rafters; low, broad, and sloping roof lines; and overhanging eaves. In Gavin Townsend's words, "'California Craftsman Tudor' might be a good description of the early houses of Charles and Henry Greene."[iv] However, as their style developed, their use of Tudor elements submerged into their own unique style, one that would come to be known nationwide as California Bungalow.

During the 1920s, Tudor houses in California lost their free, eclectic spirit and, as else-where, came to look much like those in the East. Areas around Beverly Hills and San Marino, Piedmont and Burlingame were replete with Tudor houses that would have fit in as well in Westchester or New Jersey.[v] Today, however, real estate agents in Los Angeles, at least, say they are careful to refer to Tudor houses as Country English, Tudor having lost its appeal to a preference for the more regional styles.

ABOVE: *The stained-glass tree design is characteristic of the Craftsman interest in nature.*

Robinson House

PASADENA, CALIFORNIA

Greene & Greene, 1906

THE L. A. ROBINSON HOUSE COMBINES HALF-TIMBERING with the strong horizontals developed by the Greene brothers as their style emerged gradually early in their career. They employed these elements to create a regional version of the Tudor house.

As their reputation spread, the Greenes' work began to appear in national magazines. In the January 1908 issue of *The Craftsman*, an article discussed the German character of the 1906 L. A. Robinson house. The lower floor is entirely constructed of brick covered with stucco, while the upper floor is framed in wood with stucco panels inserted between the half-timber structure. The Greene brothers combined such disparate elements as Japanese lanterns, hanging lights, the beamed roof, and a sleeping porch into a unified whole.[vi] Broad sloping rooflines with overhanging eaves and ribbon windows create dynamic horizontality.

ABOVE AND LEFT: *Gables with overhanging eaves intersect over a corner entrance. Half-timbering, projecting rafters, and a chimney elaborate the composition. An original Craftsman-style lantern lights the entrance.*

Hanging lights and Japanese lanterns were recurring elements in Greene & Greene residences.

The back of the house with its pergola and bridge entry to the dining room is newly built. Originally designed by the Greenes, it was, however, never constructed. The present owners, who have renovated and restored the house to return it as closely as possible to the original Greene brothers' design, used an empty space and the side of the house to add a terrace seen at the right. The lantern hanging from the front of the pergola, where a longer light was called for, is an interpretation of a Greene design.

Alexander House

PASADENA, CALIFORNIA

John D. Atchison, 1932

THIS HOUSE WAS BUILT IN 1932 FOR ELEANOR BISSEL of the carpet family. The influence of the Greene brothers did not appear in this Cotswold cottage–style house. Designed by Pasadena architect John D. Atchison, the house is true to its vernacular precedent of simple, straightforward lines. Constructed of rustic brick, its entrance is recessed behind an English-style porch of stone.

According to the owner, had the 5,000-square-foot house been built at an earlier time, it would have cost more. But because it was constructed during the Dep-ression, it cost only $12,000 to build. Interior woodwork is of the highest quality. The living room, dining room, and bedroom have floors of sixteen-foot mahogany planks and there are many built-ins such as shoe racks. The roof shingles are original.

ABOVE AND RIGHT: *The ivy covering adds to the picturesque quality of the country English architectural style. With rustic brick, casement windows, and its prominent steep gable, the house appears to rise as an organic part of the land- scape. Just three owners have lived there since 1932.*

Ware House

PASADENA, CALIFORNIA

Gessne & Greene, 1913

THE WARE HOUSE IS ONE OF ONLY TWO HOUSES designed by Greene & Greene in 1913. The architectural partnership would continue for another decade, but Charles was pursuing his writing and would move to Carmel within a few years, leaving Henry to do the firm's work.

Henry Ware had moved to Pasadena from Winnetka, Illinois, for reasons of health. He commissioned Greene & Greene to design a house similar to the Midwestern Tudor he had left. Henry Greene complied, although his work had long since moved in another direction. The house is not immediately identifiable as a Greene & Greene work; however, something of the firm's stamp can be found in the details.

Directly across the street from the Ware House was one the Greenes had designed in 1906. Unlike that house, for reasons of privacy, the Ware entrance is away from the street and reached along a brick walk running parallel to the house. An English look is achieved with plastering on the first story paired with shingled stories above. The second story is cantilevered above the first. The roof gable and bay windows add to the English look and half-timbering is hinted at in places. The present owner says that it had been planned for the kitchen but not added.

ABOVE AND LEFT: *The traditional English character of the house is strongest in the oak-paneled dining room, a room similar to that of the owner's Winnetka house. Henry Greene's concern for craftsmanship shows in the room's paneling and the use of cast stone and Batchelder tiles surrounding the fireplace. Mullioned windows allow ample natural light.*

In the living room Grueby tiles surround the fireplace, which is surmounted by a wire-brushed redwood mantel. To accommodate Mrs. Ware's poor eyesight, Henry Greene encircled the room with a sculptured trough of redwood for indirect lighting. The redwood continuity is carried out in the beams. Outside the living room are orange trees that date from the original land grant, and roses and wisteria planted by the Wares continue to flourish, to the delight of the present owners.

The entry or main hall, like the English medieval great hall, is an open space. The living room is to the right and the dining room to the left. An impressive staircase winds upward. The Greene interest in things Japanese is not present; rather, the room reflects an English sensibility. As in medieval houses, banks of windows light the space.

Hiner House

HIGHLAND PARK, CALIFORNIA

LIKE GREENE & GREENE, THE UNKNOWN ARCHITECT OF
this house in the Highland Park section of Los Angeles
showed a love of natural materials. And, like the
Greenes and their early work, this practitioner combined Tudor elements with those of the Stick Style,
Arts and Crafts, and Japanese influences. Constructed
of stone from the adjacent Arroyo Seco, a material
that was so much a part of the area's folk architecture,
the house is variously characterized as Stone Tudor or
as California Chalet with Japanese influences. The
gables have the steep pitch of an English gable, but
their flare bespeaks Japanese influence. The house is a
delightful example of California inventiveness and
freedom in combining elements to create the elusive
one of charm.

The decorative trim on the eaves and the rafter ends is characteristic of Craftsman use of constructional ornament work. The various elements of half-timbering, rafter brackets, and stonework combine to create a California vernacular interpretation of Tudor style.

Through its use of stone and the wrought iron of the fire screen, the living room incorporates contemporary Craftsman ideals of handicraft and appreciation of natural materials. The coved ceiling is supported on carved wooden brackets. English Arts and Crafts writers John Ruskin and William Morris, who influenced the Craftsman movement in this country, considered the gradations of color important. They would have approved the earthy tones, the yellows and greens of this room. The mural over the window combines the movement's concern for nature and its frequent use of naturalistic motifs in design.

The house was built for Edwin M. Hiner, who founded the music school at the University of California at Los Angeles.

THE NEW TUDOR HOUSE

IT IS SAFE TO SAY THAT FEW TRUE HALF-TIMBER HOUSES HAVE BEEN BUILT IN THE UNITED STATES in the twentieth century—or for that matter in England. True half-timbering consists of eight- to ten-inch-square timbers joined by mortise and tenon; the spaces are then filled with wood lath and mortar. The drawback to this method is that wood shrinks and expands with the weather, and in the less moderate temperatures of this country the freeze-thaw cycle causes the timbers to separate from the infill.

In addition, in America the use of solid timbers extending through the walls is almost out of the question because of the cost of construction and the lack of skilled craftsmen. Gavin Townsend quotes a study done by C. Matlack Price in 1915 of building materials and their relative costs: "Taking a $10,000 house as his model, Price determined that if the exterior walls of that house consisted of a typical balloon frame sheathed in shingles, the cost of the walls alone would come to $945. Clapboarding would cost $985; stucco, would be $1,171; walls built of hollow tile, would amount to $1,626; those of brick, $2,217; roughly dressed stone, $2,991. Actual half-timbered walls would come to a whopping $3,491." [i]

In England, even in the nineteenth century, authentic half-timbering was rare. In spite of Pugin's principles of "honest" construction and the Arts and Crafts movement's belief in handicraft, true half-timbering was approximated. Indeed, at British architect Richard Norman Shaw's Leyswood, which was so important to the revival of the vernacular Tudor style, the timbers, only two inches thick, are attached to a load-bearing frame. Baillie Scott, renowned architect of the Arts and Crafts Movement, set timbers less than three inches thick into brick

bearing walls. Generally, half-timbering is suggested simply by nailing thin planks to the out-side of the wall's principal material, whether stucco, brick, or stone.[ii]

For those wealthy clients who insisted on a true half-timber frame, it proved better to buy a Tudor house in England and have it shipped to America in sections and reassembled here. Others who wanted half-timbering achieved it by importing pieces of sixteenth- and seventeenth-century houses, which they incorporated into their own construction. Or they reserved the use of true half-timbering to a small portion of the house, the upper section of a gable, for example. Thus, the disadvantages of true half-timbering (and expense) were confined to a limited section of the house.

During the teens and twenties it became architecturally important that the cross braces of even sham half-timbering represent structural logic rather than merely following some fanci-ful pattern. Corner braces had to at least appear to support a weight.[iii]

Others, avoiding half-timbering altogether, chose a different substyle of Tudor house such as the Cotswold houses of Philadelphia. Henry Ford acquired a stone Cotswold cottage originally built in the early 1600s in western England and had it assembled stone by stone in his Greenfield Village museum in Dearborn, Michigan.

Today, the Picturesque house continues to be popular. Indeed, for many it represents the dream house with intimate and romantic implications. As the house in this chapter shows, it is still being built. In its contemporary version Tudor style has been tailored to today's lifestyle while retaining the elements that make it Tudor.

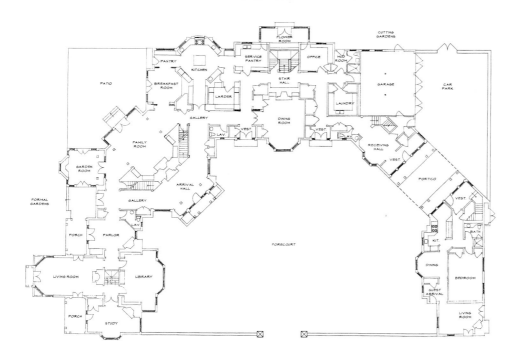

While the exterior with its slate-roofed gables, half-timbering, and clustered chimneys expresses a Tudor esthetic, the floor plan is more modern than a traditional house, although this fact is subtly hidden by the architecture. The plan is linear, open to vistas and circulation. One is always aware of different rooms through sight lines. "That," says Ira Grandberg, "is why the house comes alive when you're inside it."

Contemporary Manor House

CONNECTICUT

Grandberg & Associates Architects, Cullman & Kravis Interiors

THE CLIENTS HAD LIVED IN ENGLAND FOR SEVERAL years. When they returned to the United States and decided to build a house in Connecticut, they asked architect Ira Grandberg for a pastoral English country house, although not a traditional Tudor house like those of the 1920s and 1930s, which tended to be dark. They wanted an English house that would respond to the outdoors. "That," Grandberg says, "was the biggest challenge." He is an admirer of the English architect Edwin Lutyens's houses whose open spaces created a sense of comfortable country living. Like many of Lutyens's houses, "This house," says Grandberg, "has a Cotswold scale." Although large—22,000 square feet—it is intimate, with axial vistas oriented to the outdoors, as were Lutyens's residences.

A rare contemporary house of authentic half-

timbering, the main part of the house is true timber construction. Thanks to new construction materials of urethane panels full insulation beyond the timbers eliminates the problem of timbers shrinking from the pebbledash infill, as happened with early authentic half-timbering.

The architect had no intention of doing a historical stage set; his design is not a replication of Tudor style. Rather, it is tailored to a contemporary family lifestyle. The house is English in detail; the trim, ceiling treatment, rough textured walls, stone floors, and hand-carved stone fireplaces all bespeak English country house ambiance. The interior designers Cullman & Kravis, used a palette predominantly of green and beige to reflect, as Ellie Cullman says, "nature's surroundings of wood tones and greenery."

"The entire house is like a garden shed, responding to the outdoors and the gardens," architect Ira Grandberg says. Penelope Hobhouse and the noted English landscaper Simon Johnson carried out the landscaping, which creates the sense of being elsewhere, indeed perhaps in England.

ABOVE: *"The entire house is like a garden shed, responding to the outoors," says architect Ira Grandberg. The landscaping creates a sense of being elsewhere, indeed perhaps in England.*

RIGHT: *The double-height entry is a welcoming space with fireplace, furniture, and books. In the manner of the English Great Hall, it includes a staircase and is a space for living rather than merely circulation while also opening to other rooms of the house.*

ABOVE: *"The clients wanted a 'happy' Tudor, rather than the dark designs of the 1920s and 1930s," says Ellie Cullman. Much of the wood is limed to create a more youthful, fresher atmosphere. Douglas fir was used in the garden room rather than oak. It is filled with plants and books on gardening and uses garden-related fabric, wicker, and painted furniture. The theme of gardens is carried throughout the main rooms of the house.*

RIGHT: *The family room, designed with children in mind, is larger than the living room (not shown), which is reserved for adult entertaining. The furnishings throughout the house are comfortable in what Ellie Cullman says the English would describe as "humble elegance."*

Endnotes

INTRODUCTION
i Mark Alan Hewitt, "The Other Proper Style," *Old House Journal*, April 1997, 30.

ENGLISH TUDOR
i Gavin Edward Townsend, "The Tudor House in America: 1890–1930," unpublished Ph.D. dissertation, University of California, Santa Barbara, Chapter 1, passim.
ii Allen W. Jackson, *The Half Timbered House*, New York: McBride, Nast & Company, 1912, 2.
iii Anthony Quiney, *The Traditional Buildings of England*, London: Thames and Hudson, 1990, 20.
iv *Ibid.*, 20.
v *Ibid.*, 36–40, passim.
vi *Ibid.*, 6–8.
vii Quiney, 8.
viii Townsend, 20.
ix Quoted in Townsend, 23. Nikolaus Pevsner, "Good King James's Gothic," Hardmonsworth, England, 1928, 122.
x *Ibid.*, 25.
xi *Ibid.*, 26–27.
xii *Ibid.*, 32–36.
xiii Vincent J. Scully Jr., *The Shingle Style and the Stick Style*, Revised Edition, New Haven: Yale University Press, 1971, 8.
xiv *Ibid.*, 12–13.
xv Townsend, 36.

TUDOR IN AMERICA
i Leland Roth, *A Concise History of American Architecture*, Icon Editions, New York: Harper & Row, 1979, 232.
ii *Ibid.*, Chapter 7, passim.
iii Townsend, 41.
iv *Ibid.*, 51.
v *Ibid.*, 56, from Scully, 6–9.
vi Scully, 19.
vii *Ibid.*, 21.
viii *Ibid.*, 22.
ix Townsend, 70–71.
x Jackson, 1.
xi Townsend, 240–241.
xii *Ibid.*, 71–73, passim.
xiii Richard H. Dana Jr., "'Edgerton,' A Study in the Tudor Style," *The Architectural Record*, October 1913, Vol. XXXIV, Number IV.
xiv Hewitt, 35.
xv Townsend, 244.
xvi Roth, 225–226.
xvii Quoted in Townsend, 255: H. Vandervoort Walsh, "Houses or Stage Scenery," *Architectural Forum*, Vol. 49, November 28, 1928, 771–772.
xviii Michael Walsh, *Tudor Houses*, Farmington Hills, Michigan: Home Planners, Inc., 1989.

NEW YORK CITY SUBURBS
i Townsend, 115, taken from Frank E. Sanchis, *American Architecture: Westchester County, New York*, 1977, 3.
ii Information about Bronxville in this section is taken from *Building a Suburban Village: Bronxville, New York, 1898–1998*, edited by Eloise I. Morgan, New York: Bronxville Centennial Celebrations Inc., 1998.
iii *Ibid.*, 24.
iv Townsend, 118.
v *Building a Suburban Village*, 256.
vi *Ibid.*, 252.
vii *Ibid.*, 260–261.
viii *Ibid.*, 255.
ix Townsend, 120–122.
x *Ibid.*, 132–135.
xi *Ibid.*, 162–163.

PHILADELPHIA SUBURBS
i Much of the information in this chapter is taken from Townsend, Chapter 7, 145–164, passim.
ii *Ibid.*, 164.
iii *Ibid.*, 160.

THE MIDWEST
i Townsend, 199.
ii *Ibid.*, 199–200.
iii *Ibid.*, 201–202.
iv *Ibid.*, 206.
v *Ibid.*, 208.
vi Paul E. Sprague, *Guide to Frank Lloyd Wright and Prairie School Architecture in Oak Park*, Chicago: Follett Publishing Company, 1986.
vii Information taken from the Historic Resources Survey, City of Lake Forest, Illinois.
viii Townsend, 211–212.
ix *Ibid.*, 191.
x *Ibid.*, 192.
xi Information taken from *The Van Sweringen Influence: Shaker Heights*, City of Shaker Heights Landmark Commission, Fourth Edition, 1995.
xiii *The Van Sweringen Village*, 256.

STAN HYWET HALL
i Virginia and Lee McAlester, *Great American Houses and Their Architectural Styles*, New York: Abbeville Press, 1994. Much of the information in this section is taken from the McAlesters' book, 219–229, passim.

CALIFORNIA
i Townsend, 225, 232.
ii Roth, 211.
iii Randell L. Makinson, in Esther McCoy, *Five California Architects*, Los Angeles: Hennessey + Ingalls, Inc., 1960, 1987.
iv Townsend, 231.
v *Ibid.*, 234.
vi Makinson, in Esther McCoy, 111.

CONTEMPORARY TUDOR CONSTRUCTION
i C. Matlack Price, "The Inherent Qualities of Building Materials. An Exposition of Considerations Governing Choice, " *Arts and Decoration*, Vol. 5, September 1915, 415–18. Quoted in Townsend, 184–85.
ii Townsend, p. 185–86.
iii *Ibid.*, 187–88.